Slightly Foxed Editions

MY GRANDFATHER

&

FATHER, DEAR FATHER

SLIGHTLY FOXED EDITIONS

No. 20

MY GRANDFATHER

&

FATHER, DEAR FATHER

Denis Constanduros

First published by Slightly Foxed in 2012
in a limited edition of 2,000 copies
of which this is copy No.

232

© Denis Constanduros 1948, 1989

Slightly Foxed Ltd
53 Hoxton Square
London NI 6PB

A CIP catalogue record for this book is available from the British Library.

ISBN 978-1-906562-42-7

Printed by Smith Settle, Yeadon, West Yorkshire

Preface

In the Devon village where I grew up, the main cultural event – in fact the *only* cultural event – was the Women's Institute Drama Competition. It was held in the summer holidays, in the town hall of our local market town, and it went on for two or three days. For a child who had never been to the theatre the whole affair was magical, and excitement in the audience was intense as local WIs competed with one another in scenes from Shakespeare and, very often it seemed, in one-act plays by someone with the strange name of Mabel Constanduros. She seemed to be as much part of the whole thing as the hard wooden chairs, the interval tea and cakes, and the bus ride home through the summer-scented lanes, and I sometimes wondered who she was – a question I never pursued but which was recently answered for me in an unexpected way.

Not long after we launched the Slightly Foxed Editions, we came across a little gem of a book, first published in 1948 and long out of print, which we decided we must reissue. *My Grandfather*, as its title indicates, is a portrait of the author's maternal grandfather, who, though surviving sturdily into the reign of George V, was to his grandson a character from the 'warm, gas-lit, stable-smelling past' of the Victorian age. With delicate and affectionate humour it brings to life not only its central character, but also the world in which he lived and

5

which he surveyed with genial content from the windows of his spacious home in Kensington Gore.

The book was so delightful, so pitch-perfect in every way, it made us curious to know more about its author, Denis Constanduros – the aforementioned Mabel's nephew as it turns out – and at this point we made an exciting discovery. There was, we learned, an unpublished companion volume, *Father, Dear Father*, which, like *My Grandfather*, had once been read to much acclaim on Radio 4. We decided to publish both together for the first time, and to include some of the author's previously unpublished drawings. *Father, Dear Father* fills in, in an equally diverting way, the story of Denis's childhood in the shadow of the other important male figure in his life – his father.

The two could hardly have been more different. Grandfather symbolized everything that was convivial, straightforward and reliable. His was the very spirit of an age in which, as the author says, 'Life was simple and clear-cut. There were no complexities and half-tones.' His son-in-law Stephanos ('Steph') Constanduros, on the other hand, was flamboyant, melodramatic, full of grand ideas for solving his perpetual financial problems 'at a stroke', and inclined to take refuge from unpleasantness in ill health.

The son of a Greek political émigré, Steph had initially charmed his future father-in-law – and his future wife, who was then only 15 – with his fine voice, his singing of sentimental songs and his careless insouciance. (Once, while in full song, standing under a lighted gas jet, his hair caught fire but he continued singing 'undisturbed'. Grandfather, always susceptible to the power of music, had spontaneously clapped his hands and cried 'Bravo! Bravo!' – a gesture of approval which, as his grandson observes, he must have regretted for the rest of his life.)

In appearance Grandfather himself was 'short and round, with a face that was cherubic in its benignity'. He seemed, to his grandson, a compound of Mr Jorrocks, whom he read, admired and quoted, and his great hero, Mr Pickwick. 'As he stood at the window, chumping his false teeth slightly and perhaps whistling under his breath "Oh Rest in the Lord" or a favourite air from *The Beggar's Opera*, the likeness was remarkable.'

Grandfather's household in Kensington was certainly Victorian in its size and composition. Grown-up children had flown the nest, but Grandmother's unmarried sisters were regular guests – Aunt Maria, 'a stolid, black, unlovely figure' engaged in a perpetual game of Patience; and Aunt Pem, who was given to laughing immoderately 'until the veins on the side of her fragile head stood out in blue relief'.

Below stairs were to be found old Lucy, haunted by constant thoughts of impending disaster, and fat, jolly, carefree old Ellen the cook. The household was completed by a 'young girl', Jonzen the deep-voiced Swedish parlourmaid, and Parsons the chauffeur, who drove Grandfather to Epping every Wednesday where, much to everyone's consternation, he rode to hounds with his old friend Mr Fitch.

Images summon up that distant time: Grandfather, his feet stretched out cosily before the fire in Mr Fitch's farmhouse after a good day's hunting; stumping on his short legs through the hushed galleries of the Royal Academy to admire a favourite painting; resplendent in silk top hat at the Richmond Horse Show; perusing the obituary columns of '*The Times* Newspaper', or pouring a glass of what he called 'sherry wine'.

And sounds too: the early-morning cacophony of 'trilling sopranos, thumping pianos and scraping violins' that daily reached the household from the nearby Royal College of Music; the evening tolling of the park keeper's bell and the cries of 'All out!'; the secure and comforting sound made by the closing of the house's heavy front door – *My Grandfather* is much more than a marvellous evocation of an endearing yet tough and sometimes perverse old character. Nothing dramatic happens in it, yet everything happens – it is a meditation on an age and has the texture of life itself.

Father, Dear Father, Denis's account of his own childhood, is more like one of those comedies for which his Aunt Mabel was later to become famous. Doors open and close; characters enter and exit, and, as the action speeds up, often collide dramatically. Among them are Steph's brother Athanasius ('Uncle Ath'), a contrastingly Pooteresque, hardworking and solvent character who had married another of Grandfather's daughters, the not-yet-famous Aunt Mabel; 'Mac', the glamorous but sinisterly controlling air ace who, after the First World War, became the family's lodger; and a series of tutors employed to teach Denis and his brother – most notably Captain Wilson, who had no more interest in teaching than the boys had in learning. The main background to this tragicomedy were two hideous adjoining houses in Sutton: 'Melton', finally purchased for the family by Grandfather after

Steph – a practising but possibly unqualified architect – ran out of money; and 'Belhaven' in which resided Aunt Mabel and Uncle Ath.

Steph was a keen gardener and in summer Captain Wilson, a first-class bluffer and anxious to curry favour since his position was always precarious, would stand behind Steph's deckchair secretly consulting a rose catalogue, and engage him in conversation, throwing out knowing remarks about the roses ('Caroline Testout is a lovely climber I always think, don't you sir?'), the benefits of a dressing of bone meal and the importance of 'disbudding'. Steph was in raptures. Bluffing was a tendency shared by vivacious Aunt Mabel. If the vicar called she would be overheard earnestly discussing the efficacy of prayer, though she never went to church. 'I always give my fruitcakes a good hour and a half in a slow oven' she would tell women callers, though she never went near the kitchen.

But the greatest bluffer of all was probably Steph himself. *Father, Dear Father* is a wonderful study in self-delusion. Returning in the evening from his office in the City and sinking into the nearest armchair he would make some dramatic pronouncement.

'Well,' he would say, 'how would you all like to go to South America? A chap came into my office today and said "I want to see Constanduros – the expert. I don't want to see any of the others." He's got some big scheme to build a huge hydro-electric dam in Bolivia. If it comes off it'll be something important for all of us.'

Unfortunately the reality was very different. In hock to his bookmaker, Steph had 'a natural affinity' with all bankrupts. 'If he didn't seek them out they sought him. And some, who were financially normal when he befriended them, at once became bankrupt, as though simply to conform.'

This was a household in denial. Nothing was ever mended. 'The system in our house', Denis remembers, 'was that anything that was likely to bring my father face to face with the reality of our situation was to be stowed away out of sight.' Games of all kinds became a kind of displacement activity. The house and garden rang daily to the sounds of table tennis, a strange game called Puff Billiards, and Hoicky Hockey (played on the tennis lawn with a football and walking sticks). As relations became more strained and the financial situation grew more desperate, so the action became more and more manic, like a speeded up film.

It couldn't last, and eventually the whole farrago collapsed in a way that was both ludicrous and poignant. Fortunately, we learned from Denis's daughters, in real life there was a happier sequel. Like Aunt Mabel, with whom he initially collaborated, Denis built a highly successful career for himself as an illustrator and a writer for radio, stage and screen. How pleasingly paradoxical that such a chaotic and rather desperate childhood should have given rise to two such elegant and light-hearted little books.

HAZEL WOOD

MY GRANDFATHER

Foreword

In the early days, when my grandfather lived in his big, gloomy house on Sydenham Hill, it was my secret delight to slip away up the back stairs to the boxroom and poke about among the discarded dolls' prams and broken rocking-horses, to lift dust-sheets from antiquated furniture or broken crockery, in the hope of finding something – but what I do not know. Everything in the boxroom seemed to have a peculiar lustre and attraction. (I remember particularly well a picture of 'The Charge of the Light Brigade' with Tennyson's poem underneath. It was the *pièce de résistance* of the whole exciting show.) Every object seemed to have a new and a deeper significance for having been thrown away and rediscovered in private. Each bulging dust-sheet was pregnant with unlimited possibilities and there was a fine excitement about lifting a corner and finding, perhaps, a child's cooking stove, a pair of old riding boots, some bound magazines and a broken commode, all jumbled together in splendid confusion.

There is a very obvious resemblance between one's mind, in later years, and my grandfather's boxroom; for sights and sensations, opinions and experiences are stored away with the same haphazard abandon. As time goes by the accumulation of personal rubbish proceeds until the mental bric-à-brac of years fills the mind to overflowing with a rich and varied store of junk which can yield unlimited wealth to the careful scavenger. And there is the same excitement in lifting a corner of the memory, to find an inconsequent heap of treasures, each covered with the fictitious patina of all that has remained long under the dust-sheet. Even the useless or the downright ugly seemed alluring in my grandfather's boxroom; so it is with one's memory. Look at the number of people who swear that their school-days were the happiest in their lives. I don't believe a word of it; but I do believe that if it were possible to return from hell we should hear, not about the tortures of purgatory, but of happy days in the fiery furnace and of the sing-songs and good times enjoyed by the damned souls – all told with a veneer of nostalgic sentimentality. It is almost impossible to remember unpleasant things, at least with the surface of the mind, for the mind digests and transmutes all that it assimilates, like the stomach, and, again like it, all that is too disagreeable it generally ejects.

People and scenes recollected over a long period of time, then, are apt to have a false lustre and, seen in long perspective, one's childhood frequently has the gem-like brightness of something seen through the wrong end of opera glasses. So I make no claim that these memories of my grandfather are in any way accurate. I merely state that they are as I found them: the junk in my own personal boxroom.

Chapter I
My Grandfather at the Window

Every summer evening, at the same time, an unusual sound would detach itself from the general buzz and hubbub of traffic down Kensington Gore. It was a sound from the past, a sound of carriage wheels and horses' hoofs, a rumbling, clattering, jangling sort of a noise that contrasted strangely with the smooth, impersonal hum of taxis, buses and private cars of the late nineteen-twenties as they sped, all too efficiently, to their unpredictable destinations. As soon as he heard it my grandfather would jump to his feet from the armchair where he had been enjoying the first cigar of the day and hurry on his short, stumpy legs to the window in time to see a coach, with brasses glittering and paint newly gleaming, clatter by in the afternoon sunlight.

It was a fine sight against the plane trees of Kensington Gardens; all the finer, it seemed, for being slightly absurd – consciously absurd, but nevertheless dignified, like a ship in full sail amid dirty, utilitarian tramp steamers. It was, I believe, the last coach to run a regular service and was maintained merely at the whim of some enthusiast. It seems almost too perfect a coincidence that its route should have been right past my grandfather's front door and, consequently, his study window, for nothing could have been more appropriate or have given him greater pleasure than this sight. Nor, in their turn, could the horses, the driver and the guard have had a more critical or more appreciative audience than my grandfather, as he stood at the old-fashioned casement window which, owing to the gradual sagging of the frame, was so difficult to open, and puffed with fat contentment at his first cigar.

In appearance he was short and round, with a face that was cherubic in its benignity. With his round, red face, his silver hair and, above all, his air of happy simplicity, he seemed a compound of Mr Jorrocks, whom he read, admired and quoted, My Uncle Toby – though he had not read *Tristram Shandy* and would not, I suspect, have liked it in any case – and, most striking resemblance of all, his great hero, Mr Pickwick.

As he stood at the window with the cigar in his hand, chumping his false teeth slightly and, perhaps, whistling under his breath 'O Rest in the Lord' or a favourite air from *The Beggar's Opera*, the likeness was remarkable. Could it have been a lifelong devotion to Dickens, and Pickwick in particular, that brought it about? From early photographs he seems to have been a grave, almost sickly young man, deeply preoccupied with the labours of founding a business and providing for an ever-increasing family. (Then, in middle years, there is a photograph of him in full hunting clothes standing beside his horse in a little walled garden. What problems this poses! How did the horse get in there? Did my grandfather, with a fabulous leap, clear the high brick wall with its fruit-trees, or did he come clattering through the drawing-room and out of the french windows?) It is not until later, when wealth and position are assured, that one can see the beginnings of the metamorphosis. At first there are added the spectacles, then his whole body seems to sink and expand and there comes about him that glowing aura of genial content which is the true essence of Pickwickianism. Even his clothes were cut in a bygone fashion, for he still wore, in 1928, trousers with no turn-ups which fitted closely to the thigh and should have been strapped under the instep. Indeed, though he was the mildest and most gentle of men, he had a few most violent prejudices. One was against red-haired men, who he said were untrustworthy, and one was against boots with toe-caps. 'You might as well', he used to say, 'wear a feather in your hat as toe-caps on your boots.'

As the coach, then, passed the Albert Hall with its broad pavements and its hoardings which announced such various attractions as Symphony Concerts, Oratorios, performances of *Hiawatha* and Boxing Tournaments, the scarlet-coated guard would rise to his feet and, drawing the coaching horn from its long wicker container, would blow in honour of my grandfather such a fine, resounding, exhilarating, ridiculous fanfare: a triumphant call from the warm, stable-smelling, gas-lit past of London, that it brought my grandmother and her sisters – 'The Aunts' – to the long drawing-room window above, where they had been banished to prevent them irritating my grandfather after his day at the office. Aunt Maria would pause for a moment in her game of Patience, for the sound, connected in her mind with my grandfather who, with King Edward VII, was the only man in whom she had shown any interest, would penetrate her self-insulated brain. 'Is that the coach, Sophy?' she would ask my grandmother. An hour before she had asked: 'Is Richard in yet, Sophy?' and, content to know that he was safely home, she would continue with her Patience without further sign of animation.

But Aunt Pem, who was a few years younger, would run to the window at the first sound of the coach, laughing immoderately until the veins on the side of her fragile head stood out in blue relief. She laughed immoderately, not because she was particularly amused, but because it was the only way in which she could show emotion. Unlike most of her contemporaries she did not turn easily to tears, but turned instead to perpetual, uncontrollable giggles.

The sight of horses made her laugh more than anything, for she loved horses above all else. 'Look, Maria, you lazy old girl', she would say from the window, laughing until the tears ran down her cheeks at this fine, unforgettable sight. But Aunt Maria would sit on at her Patience, a stolid, black, unlovely figure in the soft afternoon sunlight that slanted through the glass roof of the little conservatory at the end of the drawing-room. To her it was just another coach. She had seen many coaches pass innumerable windows and they all looked much the same. She might, perhaps, make some cryptic remark about how long the run took and what time it reached certain points on its route, for she had a remarkable knowledge of un-interesting statistics and a habit of making the most bald, ungarnished statements of unimportant facts during meal times that reminded my grandfather of Mr F's Aunt, and he would quote with deep pleasure: 'There's milestones on the Dover Road' or 'When we lived at somewhere (I forget where), somebody's (I forget whose) geese was stole by tinkers.' He delighted to quote from his beloved Dickens, and my mind is full of these fragmentary, inaccurate and half-erased quotations that remind me, not of Dickens, but of my grandfather, puncturing the end of his cigar, the silver cigar-cutter held awkwardly in his short, paw-like hands, his amiable face glowing with the satisfaction of an apt quotation from his favourite author.

It was a moment of pride for my grandmother too, when the coach passed, for she was the only one of her family who was married, and this fine blast on the horn as it passed the house was a tribute, through my grandfather, to her, and thus accentuated her position of authority among the sisters.

Several times a year the Aunts were bidden from the obscurity of Croydon to stay at Kensington Gore and, though it would be unfair to say that my grandmother was patronizing, she was unable to resist the temptation to exploit small triumphs over her unmarried sisters. Thus, though it was not wartime, she forbade Aunt Maria to have more than one lump of sugar in her tea, with the result that Aunt Maria stole a supply and kept it in her handbag. Once, when drawing her handkerchief out of her bag – which she did all too seldom – she drew out with it several lumps of illicit sugar which clattered loudly all over the polished drawing-room floor in the middle of Sunday afternoon tea.

The sound of the coach, then, with its moment of triumph for my grandfather, brandishing his cigar and beaming all over his round, red face in answer to the most gracious bow, the condescending tilt of a silk hat from the driver and the passenger on the box next to him, was a moment of reflected glory upstairs in the long drawing-room with its two old ladies at the windows overlooking the Gardens and its third figure, stiff, black and incongruous in the glass-filtered sunlight of the conservatory at the farther end.

It was a moment of triumph on the next floor, too, where old Lucy, pale, thin and perpetually worried, in spite of forty years of complete security in my grandfather's household, was turning down the beds, muttering uneasily to herself, frowning at the possibility of some imagined disaster and dabbing the sheets to her puckered face to make doubly sure that they were aired. To Lucy tragedy was lurking everywhere, in every speck of germ-laden dirt, in each unaired garment or scrap of carelessly prepared food. Life for her was one long battle with the forces of darkness in an acutely domestic form.

'Tell yer Papa to mind the 'usks,' she would say, her face flushed and distraught with anxiety as she handed a plate of porridge round the dining-room screen. In her mind she was handing him his death warrant and she could foresee with awful certainty the scene in which he would drop, choking and apoplectic, to the ground, killed by the carelessness of some scatterbrained kitchen-maid. It was Lucy who decided that a purple bath mat was too bright for my grandfather and, rising suddenly from his daily cold bath, the sight of it might cause him a stroke.

Up two more flights of stairs old Ellen, resting on her bed before preparing the dinner, also heard the horn. It meant little to her. She need not go down for another half hour – 'Cook, damn you!' she would say to the chicken as she pushed it viciously into the oven – and the 'young girl' could make the bread sauce and put on the vegetables. She was the exact reverse of her lifelong friend, Lucy. Where one was thin the other was correspondingly fat; where one was perpetually shadowed by impending doom the other was jolly, carefree and unmindful of the future. 'Eat as much as you like,' she used to say to the children in earlier days, on the rare occasions when she was left to look after them. 'Here, take the sugar basin and get on with it, only for heaven's sake don't make yourself sick.' While poor Lucy would hover round, her face charged with foreboding, saying: 'Oh Ellen! Oh well, there – I don't know. No, Winnie dear, not any more sugar, dear. Tst, tst! Well there – I don't know, I'm sure.' And she would stumble out of the room on her gnarled feet, unable to bear the spectacle of her beloved children rushing headlong to destruction.

In a few brief seconds the moment had passed and the coach, clattering across the top of Queen's Gate, would diminish until it had become nothing but a faint, rhythmic beat of hoofs again, to be swallowed and absorbed in the utilitarian spate of hooting, grinding taxis, private cars and buses. Kensington Gore and the Gardens opposite, which slipped so easily into the past again, would take some moments to readjust themselves to a less picturesque present, and the ordinary everyday traffic, for some time after the coach had gone, rumbling and glittering, into the distance, would look like some grim vision of the future.

In the drawing-room my grandmother would turn away from the window to continue writing her letters, while Aunt Pem stood watching the coach out of sight as it followed the curve of the road round towards Kensington Palace, with the smile still left, forgotten, on her face. Lucy, as the hoofbeats died away, would dab the sheet to her cheek once more and mutter: 'Well there, 'tis be 'opes 'e won't catch 'is death.' Upstairs in the bedroom under the roof, with the two framed oleographs of unbelievably blue-eyed little girls with pink sashes, one called *My Mother Bids Me Bind My Hair* and the companion *When Lubin Is Away*, which Lucy had rescued from the dismantled nursery because, as she said, they were so 'sweet pretty', old Ellen would yawn and set her mind at rest for another half hour.

Glowing from the warmth of that fanfare in his honour and the condescension of those deferentially tilted silk hats, like a stone that still reflects the midday heat after sundown, my grandfather would turn back into the study, clicking his false teeth and humming to himself 'O Rest in the Lord'. Then smiling, as it always seemed, from head to foot – no great distance for him – he would stump across to the farthest, darkest recess of the study, where a tray was always placed in the most inaccessible spot, at his own request, so that he might not too easily resort to it and so that, when he did, he might feel the drink well earned, and pour himself out a first, but generous, whisky and soda.

Chapter II
Sunday Afternoon

Beside my grandfather's armchair there was a small smoker's table with, on the top, a scene, carved in soft wood, of a log cabin inhabited by bears. Half way up, just under the eaves, the cabin was hinged and the roof, folding back, allowed one to keep pipes or tobacco inside. There were several ashtrays screwed to the table outside the cabin which, owing to a surprising lack of invention on the part of the carver, were intended to look like nothing but what they were, and among these wooden bears perpetually played, while one bear, most memorable of all, stood poking his head out of the cabin door which, like a stable door, opened at the top.

The whole piece of furniture, so large for such a comparatively small use, was in a heavily Swiss-Victorian style, but to a child, as I first remember it, standing in the draped and beeswaxed billiard-room of my grandfather's previous house – a vast, Edwardian building in the forgotten backwater of Sydenham Hill – it was entrancing. The only disappointment was that, when one opened the lid to see more of the jovial bear which leaned out of the cabin door, one disclosed a contemptible deceit for, below the level of the door, where he was invisible from the outside, the bear was uncarved and merely degenerated into a block of meaningless wood. Nevertheless it was, in my mind, as indispensable an accessory to my grandfather as the white moustache or the slip-on glasses that he used for reading and which he would frequently leave upstairs in another pocket, sending one of his grandsons to fetch them with a genial: 'Thank you, my boy – when you're my age I'll do the same for you.'

It is through this table and some other relics of the past that I can best visualize my grandfather and his household in the years before I knew him. It breathes again, through its smell of pine wood and tobacco, the essence of an era which, seen in retrospect, seems like one long Sunday afternoon. There the table stood, unused, in the billiard-room, with its seats at the end raised on curved platforms, with horsehair peeling from the upholstery, on which no one ever sat. There it remained, unused and forgotten, through that long, long Sunday afternoon, while discreetly silent servants, soft-footed and whispering, flicked it with feather dusters and while the pipes of the central heating gurgled and burbled in their dutiful efforts to heat the billiard players who never came.

In summer the sunlight would stream through Venetian blinds turned down, like demure eyelids, to prevent the fading of materials or the bleaching of wood, while outside, in the wide deserted streets, a barrel organ would be tinkling gaily in the distance. A great siesta would settle over Sydenham Hill, with its large Edwardian houses behind their curving laurel-flanked drives. Outside, in those quiet, too formal gardens, the sun would succeed in penetrating the profuse but tidy shrubberies and the monkey-puzzle trees, but in the empty, elegant billiard-room there was a perpetual dim diffusion broken only by the sudden stabs of sunlight that shot straight to the parquet floor; sunlight in which the dust flecks danced and floated, to settle eventually on some surface from which, next morning, the inevitable feather duster would send them flying, swirling through space once more in an endless, meaningless repetition.

There were some photographs, carefully posed and framed, near the top of the stairs at Kensington Gore, which seemed to have captured the whole spirit of that remote period. They were taken one afternoon, at the time when my grandfather's large and various family was growing up, and they show, with a yellowing patina of decomposition, long vistas of undisturbed rhododendrons with, here and there, in cunningly contrived niches, the sightless eyes and judiciously broken limbs of statuary protruding coyly from the semi-concealment of the bushes, while in the foreground of each, frozen for all time in some spiritless game of catch or fondling a pet dog, were two pasty little girls in white dresses and black stockings.

Seeing them one longs to run through that dark, quiet garden shouting; to hack down those rank and soot-infested shrubs; to turn the hose upon those snail-smeared statues and to tell those poor, dyspeptic little girls to eat more fruit and less starch.

To visit this part of the world now is like walking through catacombs of the dead. One walks down wide roads between houses that seem to be peopled by rich, forgotten ghosts. Here is preserved, more or less intact but for a broken fence, a rotting gateway, the earthly remains of those German businessmen of the Edwardian period who made this district a little Fatherland. Here, behind lodge gates, down drives grown green with neglect, stand the seedy mansions of a past generation, as pompous as a Sargent portrait, as absurd as a hobble skirt. After the upheaval of the last war the stream of wealth and fashion shifted its bed and Sydenham Hill was forgotten, for the connoisseur an unrivalled example of Edwardian opulence in galloping decay. Now jays screech undisturbed in the shrubberies or streak across the lawns from one bank of bushes to the next, and it takes but little imagination to believe that one hears the crunching of gravel as the carriages arrive with guests for a musical evening, or a new-fangled motor-car splutters unconvincingly, dropping pools of grease on the drive. Then, as the great drawing-room windows light up once again, the noise of social clamour, swishing silk, chairs drawn back over the parquet floor, and then, in comparative silence, Elgar's *Salut d'Amour* scraped upon the violin.

Through this long Sunday afternoon my grandfather

walked, top-hatted, frock-coated, carrying his hymn book on his way to hand round the bag in church. The garden was even quieter than usual, because he would not allow croquet on Sundays in case the click of the balls should disturb the afternoon rest of his neighbours. This and my grandmother's dictum: 'Don't make a passage through the drawing-room, dears', seems to have been the only unbreakable rule of the household. He was a little preoccupied in those days, his mind still full of some business complication. 'Overheads', 'turnover', 'capital' and 'interest' would be whirling round beneath the silk hat as he walked down the asphalt path which curved, with an artlessness that Nature could not hope to rival, towards the gate at the bottom of the orchard.

There was not the full Pickwickian joviality that came upon him later as he walked down the Row in Hyde Park or examined the first crocuses in Kensington Gardens in that most beatific of all hours to a happy, God-fearing man, the hour between church and Sunday dinner. There was a peculiar attribute of sunniness about the sunshine one met with on coming out of the cellar-like coolness of church, which formal Sunday clothes seemed to accentuate. My grandfather would shuffle down the neat walks of Kensington Gardens, his top hat winking happily in the sun, clicking his false teeth slightly and humming under his breath one of the hymns from the morning service.

I can see him clearly, a small black figure with his head slightly on one side, stumping along much slower than the general stream of traffic, jostled by prams, menaced by fairy cycles, but beaming alike on everyone. Or I see him sitting on a seat beside the Row, blinking in the strong light, nodding to a friend here, raising his hat there, for he was unaffectedly pleased to see everybody and he always used to say, in his rare moments of profanity: 'It's just as easy to say "Good morning, how are you?" as it is to say "Damn your eyes."'

Chapter III
The Blue-spotted Waistcoat

Each day in the week has a special quality that is all its own and, I firmly believe, if one could be dropped at random in Time, as one could be dropped from a balloon into space, the really discerning connoisseurs of such delicate niceties could tell, merely from outward appearance, whether they had landed on a Thursday, a Monday or a Saturday. There is a busy, bustling look about Saturday morning that is unmistakable. Then my grandfather would rub his hands briskly after his cold bath in anticipation of a happy day. But for sixty years of his life Wednesday was the apogee of each week, for every Wednesday in winter my grandfather went hunting. In consequence of this, Wednesday, to me, is a day of log fires and drawn blinds, of stiff hands stretched out to warm and of steaming tumblers set beside an empty armchair.

If my grandfather was genial at normal times, on Wednesday evenings, as he stood with his back to a blazing fire, dressed in breeches, black socks, white stock and blue-spotted waistcoat, he was almost overpowered by his love of mankind in general and the whole room seemed permeated with a rosy, cosy, Dingly Dell sort of atmosphere.

In earlier days, when his good nature was more a matter of speculation, his family could depend upon the softening influence of Wednesday evening and it was then, as he drank his sherry and ate his dozen oysters – for, when they were in season, oysters were as much a part of Wednesday as the top hat and hymn-book were of Sunday – that they would stand behind his chair and ask, as casually as possible, if they might buy a bicycle or arrange a dance and, in the fullness of his Wednesday evening heart, he would say: 'Yes, my dear, of course you may. Certainly, certainly.' And he would pour himself out another glass of sherry, his stubby red hands shaking slightly with the exertions of the day and the relaxations of the evening.

The only subject which taxed even Wednesday's powers of amelioration was marriage. Though he advocated early marriages for all, especially young men, on the grounds that it was a steadying influence, and though he had been married young and enjoyed fifty years of complete happiness, for some reason these theories did not seem to apply to his own daughters. His sons he did not seem to mind about. Young men, apparently, could become engaged when and how they liked, but not young women – especially if they happened to be his daughters. On one occasion he shocked his whole family by announcing in a loud voice at dinner: 'If another man comes after one of my daughters I'll shoot him.' But this threat, though apparently never carried out, was not made upon a Wednesday. Then, if one of his daughters was imprudent enough to show him her new ring, he would merely turn his head sideways, as he did when avoiding a disagreeable subject, and say: 'I don't want to see it, my dear,' fill his mouth with another oyster and the subject would be closed – at any rate until after Wednesday.

The pack that my grandfather followed for over sixty years hunted in Essex and in early days he would drive to Liverpool Street station from south London in his phaeton. This meant starting at a chilly hour in the morning when the horses stamped and snorted, with white breath sprouting from their nostrils, and old Bob Smith on the box, his hair curling up under his hat brim like a creeping plant, was muffled to the chin in many capes, scarves and greatcoats. The whole house would be disturbed. The servants would be down early and a special breakfast cooked which my grandfather, in the spotted waistcoat and white stock, would eat in silence and alone, while outside Lucy would be fussing over his flask, repolishing the top for the fourth time or brushing his silk hat, muttering all the time to herself: 'Well, I dunno, I'm sure. Well, 'tis be 'opes 'e gets back safe, that's all I can say. But if anythink should 'appen – but, oh well, there 'tis. We've all got to go sometime, I suppose.'

Driving through the early morning streets, sitting on the box beside old Bob, my grandfather's head would gradually clear itself of the week's accumulation of business intricacies. Under the benignant influence of Wednesday morning he would blossom from a prosperous Pooterism into a racy Jorrocks or Pickwick as he jogged and swayed up the Seven Sisters Road with his hands plunged into the rugs provided by Lucy. Latterly, though the outward trappings were different, though the journey started from Kensington instead of Sydenham or Peckham and it was undertaken in a prosaic limousine instead of the more romantic phaeton with my grandfather sitting beside Parsons, the chauffeur, and not old Bob Smith, the spirit of Wednesday morning remained constant and ineradicable. In fact it grew, as the contrast between this day with its promise of a world smelling of horses and leather, a world of red faces and blue-spotted waistcoats, with the petrol fumes and dictaphones with which my grandfather was so incongruously surrounded at other times, heightened its peculiarity.

Wednesday at Kensington, as I remember it, was a day of concealed anxiety. My grandfather had ridden since he was a child without any serious accidents, so there is reason to suppose that he was at least a prudent horseman. But there remained the same doubt in everybody's mind – perhaps this day, at last, would be the one to bring trouble. After his seventieth year, naturally, the secret fears of the household increased and my grandmother openly declared that he should give it up. But grandfather, who was both stubborn and evasive on all such really important matters, always managed to put her off with a few vague, insincerely regretful remarks about it being his last season and that next year he really would be too old – though in his own mind he had no intention of giving up while he could still stand.

On Wednesday, then, after the car, with my grandfather, top-hatted once more and beaming like a child beside Parsons, with his long, pale face so exactly the opposite of my grandfather's round, red one, had slid out of sight and the front door clanked to, the household would relapse into uneasiness and irritability. My grandmother, who was always too proud to show her agitation, especially in front of the Aunts, would relieve her feelings at the expense of Aunt Pem, whose laughter would become feverish in her anxiety to please, or of Lucy, who spent Wednesdays shaking her head and muttering her expectation of disaster at the front windows, as though the fatal telegram, or better still the ambulance itself, were just round the corner.

On the very rare occasions when my grandfather did meet with a slight accident and arrived home plastered with mud and scratched about the hands and face, Lucy would be in her element. 'Well there!' she would say to my mother with a bitter laugh. 'Well there! You may think me funny, ma dear, but I can't 'elp but laugh because it's only just broke in on my thoughts as you might say. Well there, I was only saying to Ellen this morning, as I was scrubbing the kitchen table – of course I don't 'ave to scrub the kitchen table, as you know, but it's these "young girls". Really they are a pathetic treat, though I don't like to say it – not that I mind the work, of course, I don't want you to think that, ma dear – as you know I never was one to mind what I turned my 'and to and yer mother always says: "Well, Lucy," she says, "there's one thing about it you never was one to make difficulties." That's what yer mother always says and – well, as I was saying, I only said to old Ellen this morning: "Well," I said, "'Tis be 'opes nothink 'asn't 'appened to 'im because, believe it or not," I said, "I've 'ad sich a feeling 'ere all day,'" and she would lay her hand on the pit of her stomach and pause before she continued: "'Oh, Luce, you old bag of misery,' old Ellen says. But there, I knew somethink 'ad 'appened because it was jest sich a feeling as I 'ad that year I took Mr Harry to Freshwater. Well, p'raps you wouldn't remember because it was before you was born . . .' And so she would go on, slipping backwards over a compass of forty years in a sentence, then pulling herself with an effort back to the present, only to slither down the slippery slope of reminiscence once more, her face creased with recollection of innumerable domestic tragedies, so many attacks of mumps and scarlet fever, such a quantity of bicycle accidents.

While the too feminine atmosphere of the house at Kensington was charged with the accumulated undercurrents of many years, my grandfather was cantering through the keen air of Epping Forest or waiting silently at some dripping covert side for that most stirring and elemental of all sounds, the sudden baying of hounds in a hollow wood and the noise of the horn.

However much one may disapprove of hunting on humanitarian grounds or despise it for social reasons as the last refuge of an effete plutocracy, or however much one may laugh in secret at the smug little fraternity of fox-hunters with their beefsteak faces and all too simple minds, these intellectual scruples are swept aside in an instant at the first yelping, bubbling, boiling of hounds in a wood and the urgent horn, the bustle, the shouting, the sudden, blood-tingling activity of the field. The flimsy structure of humanitarianism, so laboriously acquired, collapses, as usual, like the walls of Jericho at the first blast of the bloodthirsty hunting horn. All the teachings, the theories of a thousand years are blown away in a second by the most elemental instinct of all – the instinct to kill.

Not that my grandfather, smiling genially on fox or hound alike, or any of the other normal, civilized ladies and gentlemen who were out with him, ever thought of it in this way as they galloped so gloriously over plough and through muddy woodland paths, or clattered home, chatting over the day's experiences, down darkening lanes in an air grown crisp with frost while a great, sad November sun sank below the treetops. There was no trace of cruelty in my grandfather's cherubic face or in the weatherbeaten countenance of his lifelong friend and hunting companion, Sam Fitch, whom my grandfather delighted to describe as 'a mere lad of some eighty years' and who, if my grandfather was like Mr Pickwick in appearance and character, would have served as an excellent model for John Bull himself.

Old Mr Fitch was the tutelary god of Wednesday; the warm spirit of Wednesday incarnate. For sixty years he and my grandfather had hacked home together on Wednesday evenings, warmed to the very heart with the day's sport and the knowledge that there was a hot bath waiting for them at Mr Fitch's farmhouse near Epping, and that there would be boiled eggs for tea.

Sitting in front of the roaring fire, after a bath, with the exquisite glow of fatigue in their limbs, my grandfather and Mr Fitch would renew their weekly friendship. In such a hot-house of good feeling as this it is no wonder that they should have remained the closest of friends over such a long period. It would be hard, after a day in the open air followed by a hot bath and two eggs boiled exactly to your own specifications, to quarrel with even the most diabolical character, and there was nothing at all satanic about these two extremely genial old gentlemen as they sat, eating a large tea, spluttering a little with their eggs and talking with their mouths a little too full.

'Been to any more of those "set-tos" lately, Richard?' old Mr Fitch would say in his brusque, John Bullish manner. In the sixty years during which they had been friends Mr Fitch's fortunes had remained much the same, while my grandfather, battling in the sophisticated world of commercial London, had risen to social heights that seemed dizzy in Epping, and there had grown up between them a feeling that was partly respect for my grandfather's increased wealth – the kind of respect that a schoolboy feels for a friend who has been chosen to play for the first eleven – and partly a feeling, in Mr Fitch, of pride and vicarious pleasure in my grandfather's new eminence. A speech at a public dinner, a big wedding, or a distinguished new acquaintance made in the Row, at a board meeting or at the Court of Petty Sessions where my grandfather was a magistrate, was felt as almost as much of a triumph in Epping as it was in Kensington Gore.

After Mr Fitch had swallowed, and repeated his question, my grandfather would pretend to look thoughtful for a moment, as though racking his brains to remember such unimportant things, for it would not have done to have had a list of dinners, meetings and social functions too readily on his tongue. It was necessary to the self-respect of both that they should keep up some air of casualness. 'No, Sam, no, Sam, I don't think I have,' my grandfather would answer, wiping his moustache with his table napkin and staring at the ceiling to help him remember all the various events of the past week. Then he would add, in a voice as humble and unconcerned as he could make it, 'Unless you count the Peckham Pension Society dinner at the Charing Cross Hotel and judging at the Van Horse Parade at the Botanical Gardens in Regent's Park.' And then he would be pressed into giving an account of each, of who had been present, where he had been sitting, who had been sitting next to him and what they had said.

In judging whether my grandfather was a snob because he enjoyed, and enjoyed describing, his encounters with the more exalted, one must take into account the background of the period in which he lived. For unconscious snobbery is not the true sort. In relation to our own times even the most advanced social reformers of a hundred years ago, by the lukewarmness and the condescension of their reforms, would appear detestable snobs and, no doubt, in a few generations' time the firebrands, the social revolutionaries of our day will appear as pale reactionaries, but they are social revolutionaries just the same. Snobbishness, like its opposite, is relative and must be judged as such – at least as a vice. For a man to be considered a snob in my grandfather's youth he would have had to descend to depths of social repulsiveness unimaginable now, so, if my grandfather's harmless delight in minor titles, his admiration of public pompousness, seems a little strange, one must remember that among his contemporaries he was unusually democratic and, by any standards, unquestionably humble. In fact there was something ingenuous and disarming in this attitude of respect, even though it may seem to us somewhat misplaced.

Driving back to London through the crowded, lamp-lit streets of the northern suburbs my grandfather's head would nod over his evening paper and his chin drop down on to the blue-spotted waistcoat. Alone with Parsons, who was his good friend, he could give way. If he felt tired he could show it. But as soon as the car drew up at Kensington Gore he was confronted with a whole battery of feminine eyes, as searching as arc-lights, that would scan his face for the slightest sign of fatigue. He would step jauntily out of the car, smiling broadly to reassure the eager faces pressed against the study and drawing-room windows. Was he wet? Was he unusually muddy? Had he had a fall? Even Aunt Maria, who had been saying: 'Is Richard in yet, Sophy?' until my grandmother could not bear saying 'No' any more and had gone downstairs in disgust, would rise from her Patience table at the sound of the car door and make her way slowly, brushing aside such light objects as chairs or small tables with the blind, unswerving purposefulness of an old, black tram, to the drawing-room window, where she could watch my grandfather's triumphal progress from the car to the front door.

The news of my grandfather's arrival seemed to sweep through the house as though by telepathy. Jonzen, the Swedish parlourmaid (who, when she thought nobody was looking, would throw burning matches one after another on to an unlit fire to save herself the bother of stooping), would come bustling out of the privacy of her pantry to open the front door, Aunt Pem would show her relief at the drawing-room window by laughing until her face was twisted up like a crying baby's, and Lucy, with some sewing in her hand and her forehead furrowed with care, would mutter: 'Oh well, 'e 'as come back then', with a note of bewilderment in her voice, for she was unable to visualize a safe and happy conclusion to any undertaking, even so slight a one as running out to post a letter at the top of Queen's Gate. Her eyes would watch his every movement as he jumped out of the car and waddled jauntily up the path to the front door to discover the slightest trace of a limp, and she suspected his most unconsidered gesture as having been designed specially to disguise some hidden strain or broken bone. Then her eye would light on something wrong and her voice, rising several octaves, would become almost hysterical. 'Well there, 'e 'asn't got 'is warm gloves! Tst, tst! And I put them out specially on the 'all table, that I do know because Ellen was standing just as it might be there when your mother came out of the study and said: "Oh, Luce, just run and do sech a thing," I forget now what it was, but I remember as well as anythink putting those warm gloves down beside 'is 'at. Well, if it's that young Ivy put them away again I shan't 'alf 'ave something to say to 'er. By gums, I shall 'ave to speak to 'er old fashioned, I shall really. Well, as I tell yer mother, it's not a thankful offer 'aving to train the young girls these days, it really isn't. Well, I don't know what yer puppa will think 'aving to go off like that without 'is warm gloves, because I never was one to forget anythink like that, as you know, and yer puppa always says: "Well, Lucy," 'e says, "you spoil me, you know." That's what 'e always says. Well, I shall come in after dinner and tell yer puppa that if 'is 'ands was cold it was nothink to do with me – that's all I can say.' And she would hobble off out of the room and upstairs, still muttering to herself.

At the long drawing-room window Aunt Pem would laugh until my grandfather was out of sight below the little balcony with its few dank window boxes, and Aunt Maria, having waited stolidly until she heard the front door close safely behind him, would turn and set a rigid course back to her Patience table. Only my grandmother, at the front door, the person to whom his safe arrival mattered most, would have the wisdom to disguise her relief a little and to avoid fussing round him in a too feminine display of welcome.

After a dinner in which, mellowed by fatigue, sherry and oysters, my grandfather could listen to the laughter of Aunt Pem and the curt statistics of Aunt Maria with something very near the loving-kindness that he felt for all the rest of the world, he would sit by the study fire, still in the blue-spotted waistcoat, but with his coat now changed for a velvet smoking-jacket, in a blissful Wednesday evening reverie.

Chapter IV
'Take a Dozen Eggs'

In the centre of my grandfather's breakfast table there was a silver egg-stand. It was circular with a handle in the middle, and the eggs in silver cups, surmounted by egg cosies made of flannel in the shape of chicken's heads, stood like sentinels round the outside. It was always put in the middle of the table, fully charged with boiled eggs, where it waited patiently to humour some gastronomic whim which never came; for there were always at least two other hot dishes on the sideboard, both of which were more attractive than boiled eggs. But in spite of that the egg-stand was never missing from the table and none of its eight or so cups ever appeared to be empty. It was like a religious emblem or some fetish of a simple race, put there as a sign of Prosperity, to the confusion of the evil spirit of Want, and its presence on the breakfast table was taken for granted by everybody just as much as my grandfather's own shining face as he came through the door after his cold bath and morning ride, clicking his false teeth and humming 'O Rest in the Lord'.

At lunch- and dinner-time the fetish would be there again, only this time the gods would be propitiated with custard instead of boiled eggs. There, in the middle of the table or discreetly waiting on the sideboard, would be another silver stand fully loaded with glasses. This was no mass-produced custard made from a powder, but the real thing, full of eggs. Sometimes it was plain, sometimes chocolate-flavoured and sometimes coffee, but this variation was merely an academic distinction, a gesture, because its fate, whatever its flavour, was always the same. Jonzen, the stertorous Swedish parlourmaid, would come round to each diner in succession, as though by holding the silver stand by his left ear and muttering an inaudible formula of words he would receive spiritual benefit, then return it to the sideboard where the glasses would stand, humble and forgotten, like those supernumerary flunkeys at a banquet who stand in dark corners merely waiting for someone to drop something.

The only occasion on which the egg-stand was put to use was when my grandfather had one of his younger grandchildren staying with him. Then it was always followed by the 'Boiled Egg Game', in which my grandfather delighted almost as much as the child. After the egg was eaten my grandfather would pretend to become absorbed in his paper and, with much whispering and ill-suppressed excitement, the empty shell would be put upside down in the cup and covered with a cosy. As soon as this was done my grandfather would bang his paper down on the table and say; 'Well, my boy, what I'd like now would be a nice boiled egg.' And, entering into his part as though he had never been through the familiar ritual before, he would examine the egg-stand closely as though trying to decide which one to take. This was a moment of supreme excitement. Would he fall into the trap and take the empty one or would he spoil it all by taking one of the others? Everyone round the table would watch him tensely and my grandfather, obviously enjoying the performance himself, would heighten the excitement by pretending to take the wrong one, and sometimes the child would crack under the strain and, breaking all the conventions of reality, cry out: 'No, no, Grandfather, not that one!' But whether this happened or not, my grandfather would appear to change his mind at the last minute and take the right one, saying, with a greedy anticipation that made the inevitable dénouement all the better: 'Ah now! This looks to me like the biggest.' It was an excellently built-up climax, going from one palpitating situation to another until the greatest moment of all when my grandfather lifted the cosy and cracked the empty shell with his spoon.

I firmly believe that no child was ever taken in by my grandfather's deception any more than he was by theirs. But that did not make the agony any less when he seemed about to take the wrong egg, nor did it make any less delightful the

44

grand climax when his greediness was punished and he threw up his hands and pretended to burst into tears. There was a mutual understanding between them. If one would stick to the rules and pretend to be deceived, so would the other. After all, nobody believes that Hamlet is real, and the actors know that the audience can see through their little deceptions, but no one gives the show away. Ophelia goes irritatingly mad on Monday, Tuesday, and possibly twice on Wednesday. Anyone can find her out, but they come and see her go through it all again. It was the same with my grandfather and the boiled egg.

As his grandchildren grew older even this rare use of the egg-stand ceased, but the stand itself with its load of patient eggs in their cockerel cosies remained the same. If the custom had been discontinued a feeling of deep uneasiness would have spread round the family just as it did when, after he was seventy years old, my grandfather suddenly took to marmalade. After a lifetime of jam and honey he changed. What possessed him, I wonder, on this particular morning, to break a habit of taste so long formed and open the marmalade pot after, possibly, fifty years? Perhaps it was springtime and, on his early morning ride in Hyde Park, he had found the first flowers of the horse chestnut unexpectedly open. Perhaps he had smelt for the first time that indefinable smell of a London summer which seems to be made up of blossom, smoky sunshine and hot pavements; or it may have been only a particularly big dividend. At any rate something 'shook his frail frame at eve with throbbings of noontide'. A spirit of youthful adventure came over him which crystallized itself in the form of marmalade. Not many men, I like to think, after a steady life of conservatism and sobriety, a life in which all material ambitions had been achieved, would have had enough of the old flexibility still in them to take such a step.

The effect on his family was deep. There were whisperings in the basement and in the parlourmaid's pantry. Letters sped to the married members all over the country. My grandfather, a noted abstainer, had suddenly taken to marmalade. The word flew round. It was a sign, like one of those portentous trifles that precede some great cataclysm of nature. The family waited in suspense. But nothing happened – except that my grandfather continued to eat marmalade.

When breakfast was over and my grandfather had disappeared, clutching *The Times* in one hand and his slip-on glasses in the other, I often wondered what happened to those forlorn eggs. Even in summertime, with salads at every meal, no household, however large and strange, could have found a use for eight hard-boiled eggs a day, to say nothing of the several pints of custard. I hope that they were the same eggs day after day or, better still, china ones like those used to deceive credulous chickens, but I fear that this was very unlikely.

There was an atmosphere of careless plenty about my grandfather's time that amounted, sometimes, to a kind of fatalism. Buying, to my grandmother, was a reflex action quite unrelated to needs. Her progress through a shop was queenly. She had the really vicious shopper's habit of buying first and thinking of a reason afterwards. She bought birthday presents regardless of dates and Christmas presents in May, storing them away in unlikely drawers and wardrobes where they would remain hidden for years, coming to light long after their object had been forgotten. The feeling of fatalism was strong in her, too. When one of her daughters tried to stop her buying oranges by explaining that the last dozen had gone bad she merely said: 'Never mind, dear, they'll soon be out of season,' and bought another dozen.

Seen from the precarious present this attitude seems a little shocking, like the debauchery of some oriental Croesus, but at the time it seemed natural enough and my grandfather's method of living was generally considered very frugal, for he came from an age when even the bizarre excesses of Mrs Beeton could be, and were, followed to the letter. It was a period of plethora and baroque, even in cooking, as it was in decoration. Supply was so much greater than demand that the maxim 'take a dozen new-laid eggs and a pint of the best cream, beat for half an hour and then throw away' was both possible to carry out and in every way sound economically. Eggs and cream were plentiful and the labour of the beater and the hen was cheap. Life was simple and clear-cut; there were no confusing complexities or half-tones. Those who had money could, without a pang of conscience, demand the beating up of eggs and those who had not, without hesitation or a word of criticism, would beat.

It was that blissful lack of conscience which made the late Victorian and Edwardian periods the golden age for the rich. Those were the days of wealth for wealth's sake, when richness was admired, envied and respected by all. Now, rich men, brought up in an atmosphere tinged with unconscious liberalism, creep about the countryside like lepers, jealously hiding their financial deformity. It is reasonable to assume that there is little pleasure left these days in the knowledge that one owns more than anybody should, or in watching the struggles of the less favoured to compete for the honour of supplying one with all the non-essentials of life. Wealth is no longer fashionable and even the comparatively affluent will go to great lengths to prove that they are on the point of bankruptcy and that all their possessions are quite valueless. This is a revolution of considerable importance which has come about in our time and in our midst, with scarcely a word of recognition from anyone. My grandfather's egg-stand, like so many of the eggs it once held, is in the dustbin once and for all.

Chapter V
Noises and Places

Whenever I recall my grandfather I think of him chiefly in the evenings. There was something in the comfortable relaxation of the evening, after a busy day, that clearly epitomized my grandfather's character as I remember him. He probably preferred the morning, with its cold bath and ride before breakfast, but I like best to think of him sitting in his armchair after a good, though not necessarily large, dinner, puncturing the first cigar of the day with a look of expansive beatitude on his face and '*The Times* Newspaper' as he always called it – for he came of a generation which also had the leisure and energy to speak of 'sherry wine' – folded across his stumpy legs.

In earlier years he would sit up at night and read adventure stories in order to be able to re-tell them to his grandchildren in the morning. When my brother and I were dressing we would hear his singsong voice calling to us down the long, unlit passages of the house on Sydenham Hill, and we would hurry off to his dressing-room and sit, rapt in attention, while he shaved himself with a cut-throat razor before his old-fashioned shaving stand and told us haltingly, with pauses for shaving, the story of three characters called Ralph, Peterkin and Jack in *The Gorilla Hunters*, or gruesome tales of lions from a book called *The Man-eaters of Tsavo*. Told by my grandfather, still fresh from his cold bath and morning ride, the stories seemed to gain a new actuality that made them far more absorbing and memorable than anything merely read aloud. One always had the feeling that grandfather himself had met one of the notorious man-eaters lurking among the rhododendrons of Dulwich Park.

There is an easy, rather obvious sentimentality about the evening which suited my grandfather and his generation admirably. Those were simple days when a painter could be satisfied with the facile emotionalism of syrup-like sunset or the depiction of old age, and any artist with the dash and courage to include both on the same canvas was almost sure of an admiring crowd at Burlington House. My grandfather might almost be said to have included both in his own person, as his genial red face was like a setting sun and he carried an aura of evening comfort and accomplishment, of glowing fires and placidity with him as naturally as a snail carries its shell.

For that reason my mind slips back most easily to the

picture of my grandfather beside the study fire, his short legs stretched out stiffly on a hassock, like a child who cannot touch the ground, and his gouty fingers fumbling with his after-dinner cigar. The tray with the whisky and the soda-water, which nobody but he ever drank, is in position on the study table, as far as possible from my grandfather's chair, and the dull London traffic rumbling by outside the curtained windows with a sound so incessant as to be almost inaudible after a time, like the noise of a waterfall or of the sea to those who live within earshot of them, adding a feeling of security, by contrast, to the comfort of the room. Or perhaps it is a summer evening. My brother and I take it in turns to read aloud *The Pickwick Papers* or *The Fortunes of Nigel*; for my grandfather had an unfortunate fondness for the slow-motion romanticism of Scott; and as we read, park-keepers in the gardens opposite are beginning to chant: 'All out' and toll their hollow hand-bells.

Sitting in the fading light by the study window and following – or failing to follow – the tortuous fortunes of Nigel, the sound had a peculiar quality that stays in the memory. It seems now to be the key to that whole period, something peculiar both to the place and to the time, as the hooting of tugs on the river does to those who have once lived in Chelsea. If it were possible to play back in one's mind a record of those park-keepers with the exact intonation of the chanted 'All out' and the tolling hand-bells, first from somewhere nearby and then thinly, as a counter theme, an answering shout from far away in the gardens where a white mist is beginning to rise under the trees, I feel that I could recapture one instant of time in the round, instead of flatly, in the two dimensions of memory, and that I could actually hear the splutter of my grandfather's syphon as it emptied or smell the peculiarly dusty smell of the green plush cloth on the study table.

There are other sounds which, to a lesser degree, have the power to evoke the period, such as the shutting of the heavy front door and the sudden diminution of traffic noise which always brought with it the elemental feeling of seclusion and security: of being unassailably remote from the world. Then there was the early morning noise to which one woke. The practice rooms of the Royal College of Music were close behind my grandfather's house and the first sound that one heard on waking up was a babel of trilling sopranos, thumping pianos and scraping violins, a chaotic pattern of scales, repeated phrases and sudden cadenzas that was as thrilling as the tuning-up of an orchestra or as the busy tumult of birds at daybreak and which always gave one an indefinable feeling, as one lay half awake, that the curtain was about to go up on a day full of the promise of good things.

But neither of these so exactly suits the period as the muezzin-like wailing of the park-keepers at closing time. I can see my grandfather, a lonely black figure in the encroaching darkness, trotting in complete solitude towards a locked park gate – for the sound of those keepers and the knowledge that the Gardens were closing always roused some imp of perversity in him and he invariably entered the Gardens very slowly, just as everyone else was hurrying to the gates. In a few moments the crowds would melt away, the twisting paths would be empty except for this one figure, moving very slowly

and apparently oblivious to everything. The cries of the keepers and the ringing of their hand-bells would begin to sound
from all directions like lights snapping on in the darkness, but
still he would move on, a solitary figure in a depopulated
world, until at last he came to a gate where he would have to
tip the porter half a crown to let him out.

Chapter VI
My Grandmother Pulls a Face

On the morning of my grandparents' golden wedding, Lucy, bringing them their early morning cup of tea and the two regulation pieces of thin bread and butter, greeted them by saying: 'Well I can't say *many* 'appy returns of the day, I suppose, but 'tis be 'opes with care – and cheerfulness – we might say a few.'

My grandmother was angry about it because she did not like being reminded of the fact that she could not expect many more 'happy returns', but grandfather went off for his early morning ride delighted to have another anecdote to tell his grand new friends in the Row. Their attitude towards age was different, partly, no doubt, because my grandfather's health was always robust, while my grandmother was for many years in that precarious state when one slight illness – a cold not shaken off or an attack of bronchitis – would have made her a permanent invalid. Living in a house with old people has its disadvantages. There are so many topics that cannot be discussed, so very many taboos. One's mind becomes unnaturally agile in anticipating any topic that may lead, however indirectly, to a reference to the future. Merely remembering the past becomes a sterile occupation when it is not accompanied by anticipations of the future.

My grandfather's own attitude to old age was mixed, but when he was over seventy he developed a great personal pride in his own age and was only too eager to tell everybody how old he was. He acquired a record-breaker's outlook and, in order to make himself out as old as possible, even went to the length of adding a year by saying, when he was seventy-five, that he was in his seventy-sixth year. There is a jealous rivalry among the really old. This made things very difficult when dealing with my grandfather, because to mention anyone who was several years older than himself and still active, while it was a compliment in that it implied that he was comparatively young and had many years before him, was a mortal insult to his professional pride as an Old Man. If he was to be old at all, then he would be older than anybody else.

Sometimes, when he was in the mood to be considered young, he would look down the Deaths column in 'The Times Newspaper' until he came to the announcement of somebody considerably older than himself and he would read it out with obvious satisfaction, starting off with the words: 'Well now, here's a poor young chap cut off in his prime.' Then he would read on gaily: 'At Elmbank, Tranmere Road, Wimbledon Common, Nathaniel Prangle, in his ninety-third year . . .' And he would take another piece of toast and marmalade, encouraged by the thought that, to Nathaniel Prangle, floating about in the cosmos, he must appear a mere child.

It seems strange that anyone so cheerful, so essentially alive and in full enjoyment of this world as my grandfather appeared to be after his cold bath and his morning ride should have breakfasted regularly off obituary notices. Perhaps it gave him a twinge of malicious satisfaction while sitting at the breakfast table, glowing with his recent exercise, and still experiencing the mundane pleasures of hot tea and toast too thickly buttered, to read of those who had failed to remain alive any longer. At any rate he took what appeared to be a morbid interest in the death of anyone he had known, however slightly, and was an eager and conscientious attender of funerals. Breakfast, though it still contrived to be a cheerful meal, as any meal at which my grandfather presided would have been, was always eaten to the accompaniment of a list of names of the recently dead, reverberating round the room like the tolling of a bell.

My grandmother, who probably thought more about death itself, did not share his keen interest in the dead and cut him short one morning in the middle of his reading by saying that she thought it was selfish of old people to die after a long illness. Why couldn't they die before and save their relations all the trouble? Grandfather was disgusted at this frivolous and illogical point of view and from that day onward, whenever he came to the words 'after a long and painful illness bravely borne' he would say: 'Ah, another selfish chap, I see,' with a bitter intake of breath through his white moustache.

Obituary notices were not his only breakfast-table reading. During the Great War he would read at length extracts from *The Times* about the military position. It was a pity for my grandfather, as for many other Englishmen of his generation, that the war was fought in France. Almost any other country would have been better, for he could not bring his Anglo-Saxon lips to form the mincing, emasculate sounds made by Frenchmen. It seemed to him a sign of embarrassing affectation to pronounce French place names correctly so, like his often-quoted friend Mr Boffen, in his readings of *The Rise and Fall of the Roman Empire* ('the old "Rise and Fall off the Rooshun?" Why I ain't been right slap through him lately,' etc., etc.), he would crash his way through one obstacle and, before he could recover his mental balance, he would be confronted by another. And so he would go on, frequently stumbling, sometimes hesitating and often reduced to using sheer brute force, but never beaten, while my grandmother, sitting at the other side of the table, unseen behind the paper, would make absurd and disrespectful faces at him as a kind of running accompaniment.

If by any mischance he had lowered his paper at the wrong moment and seen those faces he would have been utterly at a loss to understand them. In his own mind he had built up an entirely fictitious character for my grandmother, composed of all that was fine and noble in womanhood, or at any rate all that was considered fine and noble in womanhood during the latter half of the last century. To him she was not a mere human being but a Dickens heroine, and who could imagine Dora squinting and putting out her tongue behind David Copperfield's back, however laudable such an action may seem nowadays? But who knows, perhaps Dickens's heroines were human after all, like my grandmother, in their off moments? Even Little Nell, when she was not catching her author's eye, may have given way to some minor vulgarity – at least let us hope so.

The trouble with my grandfather and his contemporaries was over-simplification. To them heroes were perpetually heroic, twenty-four hours in the day, and villains as persistently evil. There were no half tones, no gradations from good to bad. They had a tendency to divide humanity quite simply by two in all matters, whether actual or metaphysical. Their world was conveniently composed of Beauty and Ugliness, Radicals and Conservatives, God and the Devil, Oxford and Cambridge. It was a simple world.

Fortunately for my grandfather he never lowered the paper in time to see those disquieting grimaces, and so he remained, for the fifty-two years in which they lived together, pleasantly and sentimentally ignorant of at least half his wife's character; for those grimaces were significant.

They were significant of my grandmother's rebellion against the humdrum routine of a materially easy life and were part of that curious urge which forced her, during many long summer afternoons, to drive round Surrey looking at houses which she herself knew quite well would never be taken. There were at one time hardly any largeish houses within a radius of twenty miles of south London outside which I have not sat with Parsons for many weary hours playing our own specially invented game of cribbage with the number plates of passing cars, while my grandmother, sometimes reluctantly accompanied by grandfather himself, would trail round the garden seeking an unattainable, a non-existent Perfect House. As my grandfather prospered, so these house-hunting Odysseys grew more frequent and less satisfying to my grandmother until, in the words of her family, she could be content with nothing less than a shady desert.

All this was implied in those faces behind the morning paper if my grandfather had but seen them, but he did not. He remained, as I have said, in a state of pleasantly sentimental ignorance until she died. After her death his sentimentality flourished unchecked, though, with a complexity of motive that must have been confusing to himself, his first action was to write to the newsagent and stop the periodicals which my grandmother took and his next was to pay for her funeral out of the money in her banking account. For, though he was obviously overcome by grief and emotion, he was at all times that most un-Dickensian mixture, a practical sentimentalist.

Chapter VII
The Grey Bowler Hat

One evening when my brother was having dinner alone with my grandfather (these *tête-à-tête* dinners, by the way, which they had frequently at the time, were nearly always spoilt by the fact that my grandfather had bought a bottle of orange bitters at Harrods. Someone among his new friends had recommended him to do so and, brought up as he was on sherry and port wine, he drank it in a glass neat, and my brother, out of ignorance and respect, did so too. There was a great fuss made of opening the bottle and taking the first sip. They both drank together and then paused in silence while Jonzen, the Swedish parlourmaid, breathed with gusty obsequiousness in the background. They paused. The drink was nauseating. There was no way out now. It had been recommended by someone who knew what was what, it had been ordered specially from Harrods, brought to the dining-room, examined, opened and tasted in impressive silence. After such a preparatory fanfare there was nothing left but to like it. 'Well, my boy,' said my grandfather, smiling bravely, 'what do you think of it?' What could my brother say? My grandfather refused to be beaten. Every time they were left to dine alone he would say, as though it was a special treat: 'Well, my boy, what about a glass of orange bitters?' And each would know, with a heavy heart, that they were condemned to a meal of misery.)

As I was about to say, one night when they were dining alone together my brother suddenly said: 'Why don't you buy a grey bowler?' At first my grandfather was dubious about such a break with established precedent, as he had worn nothing but a black silk hat on Sundays – and Wednesdays in the hunting season – or a black bowler on all other days for a long lifetime.

The uninitiated may feel that there is a merely academic distinction between a black bowler and a grey one. Each, they may argue, is a hat. They are identical shapes, even the colour is only a difference of tone. What ignorance! One might as well argue that there is no difference between Beethoven's Choral Symphony and 'Pop Goes the Weasel'. Each is music, each based on the same fundamental laws of construction, but it would be as impossible for the average black-bowlered city clerk to whistle the Choral Symphony from beginning to end as it would be for him to change his bowler to a grey one. He would not lose his job, no doubt, nor would his wife leave him. The tradesmen, in all probability, would not ask for an immediate settlement of their accounts. In fact, there would be no disastrous consequences, such as those which bring obedience to the laws of man. In spite of this a force far stronger than the threat of imprisonment prevents him performing the simple and quite legal act of buying a grey bowler hat, even if it is his one consuming desire.

It would be useless and tiresome to attempt a learned and pompously scientific explanation of this force, though no doubt it could be done by psycho-pathological research in a mere matter of a few hours and an answer given as neat, as shapely and as tasteless as an algebraic equation. We need go no deeper into the question than to say that it is the force which makes elephants act like elephants and Chinamen like Chinamen. It is the force which prevents a tram from behaving like a bus, for there are prescribed limits to the actions of individuals which may not be exceeded except by those rare personalities with sufficient strength to break these pre-natal bonds. Obviously anyone with these special qualities would not remain long a city clerk.

Therefore when my grandfather debated the question of buying a grey bowler he was contemplating a far greater step than he realized. Only a man who had had the courage to take to marmalade late in life would have considered it for a moment. For some days the subject was dropped, while my grandfather's imagination toyed with the idea, then, one night after dinner, the decision was taken. He would buy one.

Lucy, who always bought his clothes for him – half a dozen shirts at a time, all alike, a box of black or dark blue ties, a dozen pairs of black socks – was sent to the hatters to select a number to be sent on approval. The next evening, when dinner was over, my grandfather and my brother retired to the study in suppressed excitement to try them on. There they lay on the round study table, some in boxes, some in virginal tissue paper: four gleaming, unsullied, seductive grey bowler hats. What a scene it must have been in front of the study fireplace, with my grandfather whistling 'O Rest in the Lord' under his breath in an attempt to show that trying on a grey bowler was an everyday matter and scarcely worth a moment's interest.

It is hard to say whether the grey bowler was a symptom or a cause of the change, the expansion, that took place in my grandfather during the last few years of his life. During the period in which he was building his business there was little time to consider whether he had any tastes beyond work, and no time at all to indulge them if he had. But latterly, in the mood induced by the wearing of the grey bowler hat, he developed a keen interest in cricket and the Royal Academy.

He would leave the office slightly early on fine summer evenings and drive, perhaps, to Burlington House, where he had a season ticket, and spend a happy hour in that sedately hushed atmosphere, stumping from room to room with his marked catalogue open, revisiting favourites, pausing here to admire a particularly succulent landscape, and there a flashing equestrian scene. Or he would tell Parsons to drive him to the Oval and they would bowl down the Vauxhall Bridge Road faster than they went towards Piccadilly, because Parsons was a cricket enthusiast himself and if Somerset happened to be the visiting side the rivalry between him and my grandfather became acute.

Inside, on the hard benches of the members' stand, my grandfather would doze through many an hour of content-ment while the slow white figures moved to and fro in the smoky sunlight of late afternoon. There is always a pleasant drowsiness about a cricket match towards the end of a long day's play, when desultory applause ripples round the ground like little waves on a hot beach, and though my grandfather was a comparative newcomer to the Oval and to cricket in general, the mellow atmosphere of the place suited him admirably. He would sit there nodding like any hardened habitué, until some spectacular piece of play – a catch on the boundary or a particularly lusty hit by one of his heroes, for it was in the great days of Surrey cricket, when the side included Hobbs, Sandham, Fender and Strudwick – roused him to a state of unrestricted enthusiasm that must have branded him at once as a mere amateur of the game. He felt, too, the proper schoolboy veneration for the long refreshment room in the pavilion, with its photographs of the famous and its air of determined ugliness, and for the steps down which so many illustrious boots had clanked on their way to the wicket.

The grey bowler had another, indirect effect also. He took to the theatre. For many years he had not been to anything but an occasional oratorio, of which he was extremely fond – in fact, he never missed a performance of *Elijah* or *The Messiah* and kept a kind of score card in his memory of the number of times he had heard them. But the theatre came as something completely new to him. *The Beggar's Opera* became his chief favourite and the Lyric Theatre at Hammersmith was as much his haunt as Burlington House or the Oval, and he would sit in his stall, beating time to the familiar tunes with both his short, gouty hands, like a delighted baby. In fact, my grandfather's whole approach to the theatre was child-like in the extreme. He was so inexperienced a theatre-goer that he came to it with a child's eye and was happily deceived by everything. No conventional phrase was too threadbare and no plot too banal to please him, for he had seen none of them before. He was the perfect audience and, on some occasions, must have exceeded even the wishes or intentions of authors, actors, producers and management, for once, at the end of the second act of a musical comedy, when the heroine in a white frock stood among the cardboard clematis to sing a routine sentimental number about the apparent faithlessness of her lover, my grandfather, who could not bear to see a woman unhappy, especially after dinner, burst into tears.

Chapter VIII

'A Few Oughts'

Some of my grandfather's quotations from Dickens were developed and amplified into the form of small dramatic performances in which the whole table took part and gave their allotted responses. There was one special favourite from *The Pickwick Papers* which went, as far as I can remember, like this:

MY GRANDFATHER (*pouring himself out another glass of sherry*): 'What was the last thing you devoured?' says the doctor.

MY BROTHER: 'Roast beef,' says the patient.

MY GRANDFATHER: (*pausing with the glass in his hand*): 'What arter that?' says the doctor.

MYSELF: 'Crumpets,' says the patient.

MY GRANDFATHER: 'That's it,' says the doctor.

MY BROTHER: 'What's it?' says the patient.

MY GRANDFATHER: (*through the sherry glass*): 'Crumpets,' says the doctor.

MY BROTHER: 'But crumpets is 'olesome,' says the patient.

MY GRANDFATHER: (*hanging down his empty glass*): 'Crumpets is *not* 'olesome,' says the doctor, wery fierce.

This was the *bon bouche* we had all been waiting for. It never failed to bring the house down and was the juiciest line in the whole performance. My grandfather put all he knew into those stirring words, 'Crumpets is *not* 'olesome,' and I can hear his chuckle of satisfaction now after 'wery fierce', as he beamed round the table in the dull glow of the lamp from the sideboard. It did not matter in the least that we had been through the whole performance the evening before and would undoubtedly do so again the next day. In fact there is something comforting about repetition for its own sake, especially to the ingenuous and unwary, as all concocters of propaganda, from religion to politics, know. The human mind takes kindly to repetitions. One has only to say a thing often enough and the critical faculties, lulled by the tom-tom-like rhythm of sound, will accept it without a murmur. The very fact that my grandfather had said those words so many times before made them seem part of his daily life and one of his necessary comforts, like the glass of whisky and the after-dinner cigar.

In spite of his bold decision to buy a grey bowler and his taking to marmalade my grandfather was at heart a confirmed ritualist. He rose at the same hour every morning and trotted off to his cold bath, dressed in long pants which made him look more like Mr Pickwick than ever, and at exactly the same moment every day he would cross the road and mount his horse from the mounting block just inside Kensington Gardens.

He was greatly helped in all this by Lucy. She was an arch ritualist. Whenever my grandfather went away for a holiday, which was as seldom as he could manage, she would arrange his room to be as nearly a replica of his study at home as she could make it: an armchair, with *The Times* folded over one arm, would be placed at the same angle to a smoking table as his chair at home. In fact everything would be done to make him forget that he had gone away at all. This was largely to shield him from shock, which, to Lucy, was inseparable from all forms of change and extremely dangerous to the system. Therefore change, in any form, was a thing to be avoided at all costs. (That was why, as I have said, she removed the purple bath mat from my grandfather's bathroom. It was replaced with one the colour of quiet mud.)

The satisfaction that my grandfather felt, then, when he declaimed the words: "'Crumpets is *not* 'olesome,' says the doctor, wery fierce,' was a good, natural and primitive feeling. It was much the same as a native craftsman must feel after having repeated the same pattern for the five hundred and sixty-fourth time or a priest on uttering a familiar formula of words.

It was the number of times he said it that pleased him. There is always something mesmeric in high numbers, as my grandfather knew himself, for, if he happened to glance through one of the less sober newspapers which occasionally found their way on to the breakfast table, and saw a lurid headline such as '50,000,000 Die in World's Most Terrible Tornado', or some other soothing story of other people's troubles, he was not taken in for a moment. 'Chah!' he would say, putting down the paper in disgust, 'What are a few oughts to a newspaper man?' and he would revert to his *Times,* which would put the whole cataclysm in its place by merely mentioning it on an unimportant page, among meteorological reports, as 'High Wind Velocity Recorded in Parts of Patagonia'.

The mesmerism of high numbers is perfectly illustrated in Military Tattoos. Huge crowds will come from great distances in the middle of the night to see a thousand men doing at once what nobody would walk across the road to see one man do by himself. If one man wants to swing an Indian club that is his own business and nobody will be sufficiently interested even to try to stop him, but if a thousand men should swing Indian clubs together, then large sums can be charged for the pleasure of seeing them. A thousand times nought – or as my grandfather would have said 'ought' – is not 'ought', as any newspaper man knows, but about a million.

Chapter IX
The Richmond Horse Show

Some time in June the Richmond Horse Show was held and the Coaching Club met at the Powder Magazine beside the Serpentine. In my recollection it was always the sunniest day of the year, though this may be because, for some unknown reason, it was to me one of the most exciting. Whether my memory has succeeded in editing the facts and excluding all occasions on which the Coaching Meet was held in the rain or whether the explanation is simply that we did not go when it was wet I cannot say. I only know that every time I cross the bridge over the Serpentine and pass the low, pleasing exterior of the Magazine I am transported into a world of sunshine and new paint, of stamping horses and clinking harness: a world in which all the women wear new summer dresses and the men carnations in their buttonholes. All, that is, except me.

The day of the Coaching Marathon was always a great one for the household at Kensington Gore. For days before Lucy would be preparing my grandfather's clothes, pressing and ironing, muttering to herself like a soul in torment, brushing his silk hat and then replacing it in its white box on the top of the cupboard in the downstairs cloakroom, where it would be safe from the infidel hands of the 'young girls'. 'Well there, 'tis be 'opes no one don't touch 'is 'at because 'e always likes me to get 'is things ready for 'im, that I do know. 'E always did say: "Lucy," 'e says, "there's no one can get a shine on a silk 'at like you can," 'e says. I can remember 'im saying that as well as anythink many years ago. Well, it must 'ave been a long time ago because I was just as it might be here on the stairs, taking up Mr Reggie's tray with 'im in bed with the chicken-pox – or was it when Miss Marjory 'ad whooping cough? Tst! Well there, I forget. No, it couldn't 'ave been Miss Marjory be-cause that was the year yer granny took the 'ouse at 'Ind'ead. Oh, that was a nice 'ouse! As soon as I saw it I said: "Well there! That's what I call a really nice 'ouse." I don't mean ter say that yer granny didn't always take nice 'ouses. She always took the best and that we know, but that little 'ouse at 'Ind'ead was sweet pretty . . .' And her voice would trail on to an invisible audience when one was two flights up the stairs.

On the great day itself there was a special quality even about the noise from the practice rooms of the Royal College. I am sure that, lying in bed with one's back to the window in the half-conscious stage between sleeping and waking, one could tell from the thrilling cadenzas of the violins, the sudden cascade of notes from the pianos and the exuberant contraltos that it was a sunny morning and that something unusually good was to happen during the day. It was one of those days when the most familiar sounds, taxis hooting, the grinding of buses as they started away from the bus stop across the road, all seemed charged with a special significance, were all part of a pattern of sound, an overture to great things.

Downstairs the activity was tremendous. Sandwiches were being spread and cut, meat pies packed in greaseproof paper and the inevitable bottles of tonic water and ginger ale, as well as something stronger for my grandfather himself and any of his distinguished friends who might be entertained, squeezed into picnic baskets that were an excitement in themselves. (Anybody who can resist the sight of a well-filled picnic basket and all it implies is, I solemnly state, dead to this world and ripe for the next.) Jonzen hurried in and out of her pantry on mysterious errands connected with bottles and glasses. In the basement Ellen, with sleeves rolled up and, probably, a glass of stout under a dish cover, was directing operations among 'the young girls', while Lucy ran to and fro between them all, up and down stairs, pressing, polishing, cutting, packing, fitting in, pulling out: in fact, performing every domestic feat known to woman, all within the space of a few moments and all with a face seamed with woe and a voice two octaves higher than usual to mark the importance of the occasion.

The arrangement for the day was that we should all congregate at the Magazine in the morning to see the Meet and to watch the coaches start. When the last one had gone we should drive down to Richmond with Parsons in time to see them arrive. My grandfather, who acted as an umpire, went down on one of the coaches while we, with the lunch basket, hurried on to get there first.

It was a fine sight at eleven o'clock on those June mornings in front of the Powder Magazine. It was too early in the day and too early in the year to be really hot. The sun did not beat up from the asphalt pavements with the vitiating power of late July or August and the new green of the trees was not yet dulled and dishevelled by the dust of a long London summer. Everything was new, fresh and full of promise. Everything perhaps, except the odd, horsey old gentlemen in their grey top hats and their shepherd's plaid trousers. Neither they nor their anachronistic pastime were either new or particularly fresh, except in glinting paint and brass, and certainly not full of promise. Indeed, it would have been hard to find a more completely lost cause or a more hopelessly irrelevant gathering of human beings in the country than those buttonholed old gentlemen and their elegant, exquisite women. Fortunately for me I was able, in those days, to look on them in a spirit of detachment. My eye was unclouded by the cataract of a social conscience and, in my ignorance, I was able to enjoy the spectacle for what it was worth. I enjoyed it with the simplicity of a baby or an artist, for to each it is the appearance of a thing that matters; its shape, colour, sound and smell. There are not a whole dead weight of consequences and implications attached, like weeds round a swimmer's legs, to everything seen. They are more interested in the colour of a thing than its price, how it was made, who made it and how much per hour they were paid to do so. At least they should be, for if they are not they are no longer babies – or artists.

We arrived at the Meet, I think, separately from my grandfather. This was to be his day. As an umpire and the owner of a coach, though it was the property of his business and not privately owned like the very best coaches, he was so exalted and so greatly superior to the rest of the family that we came humbly by ourselves, not daring to catch his eye or to look as though we might belong to him as he stood out in the middle of the road among the fine horses and the strange, ramshackle old gentlemen who seemed so impressively distinguished when viewed from the respectful distance of the kerb. There he stood in the middle of it all, smiling on everybody, exchanging a word here and there with someone whose picture one had seen in the society papers, while we, watching from the less colourful crowd on the pavement, pretended, if he should turn our way, to be very busy looking in another direction, so that he should be spared the embarrassment of having to acknowledge us.

There was a tacit agreement between us, like the arrangement between brothers at school, that we should not take advantage of our connection or presume sufficiently to expect recognition, but I can remember hoping secretly that he would come over to the kerb in his splendid horsey clothes with his membership badge dangling from the lapel of his coat, and say just a few words so that we should be elevated above the rest of the crowd pressing round us or, better still, that some gilded gentleman from the box seat of one of the coaches might recognize us as his relations and raise an exquisite hat.

Generally my grandfather would come across to see us and sometimes even introduced us to one of his friends, for an acquaintance in the Row had reported favourably upon us, but if by chance or design he failed to see us in the crowd I was reduced to seeking out the business coach and making myself known to old Bob Smith, the coachman, who, as a life-long employee of my grandfather's was bound to touch his hat respectfully.

At eleven o'clock there would be a general stir among the knowledgeable and privileged few and among the coaches drawn up on either side of the road. An especially gorgeous gentleman would begin running up and down the road, calling out, gesticulating, ushering away the crowd and, amid the clicking of tongues and unrhythmical stamping of hoofs, the first coach would rumble into movement. Everybody would stand back and cast appraising eyes over the turnout. The driver would raise his whip with a flourish, in every direction hats would be tilted and the guard would rise in his seat and blow a brave, triumphant fanfare. The sun shone and glinted on new paint and polished brass, on silk hats and summer dresses as the first coach rattled magnificently away over the bridge across the Serpentine and was lost in the traffic.

The starter would look at his watch and, after a few minutes, the whole process would begin again, and so on, until the last coach had rumbled into the distance and the space in front of the Magazine seemed emptier than ever before. Then the crowd would disperse until there were only a few nurses with perambulators or groups of children with tiddlers in a jam-jar and we would walk home again through a park humming with the gathering momentum of a summer day.

This, though possibly the best part, was only the beginning of the day's activities. There was the drive down to Richmond, beside Parsons, the arrival on the ground and the excitement of finding one's allotted parking place, and then, on getting out of the car beside the judging ring, that peculiar smell of trampled grass and hot humanity which transports one instantly into a world of race meetings and Bank Holidays. There we would sit, eating the superabundance of sandwiches, patties and salads, while a seemingly endless succession of horses trotted, cantered, galloped or merely walked round the ring to the sound of 'Light Cavalry' or 'The Blue Danube' from a military band in the centre.

I do not know why this day should have had such a fascination for me at all other times of the year. I did not ride and knew nothing about horses. As the long afternoon dragged by and the meaningless succession of horses paraded round the ring or waited for what seemed hours before the judges, I would sit in the car in my unsuitably stiff clothes, while the upholstery of the seats became so hot that one could not bear to touch it. Gradually, as I drowsed in the front seat of the car and the noise of the band, fluctuating with the distance, came in intermittent gusts of sound, I experienced the annual disillusionment that this was, after all, an exceptionally boring day. It was like the yearly disappointment of Christmas, which I always looked forward to all the year round. It was not until it actually came that I experienced once again that peculiarly seasonal ennui which reminded me that Christmas was no longer what it used to be. Sitting in the car through the long afternoon I would have the feeling that this year the magic of the Horse Show had failed to work, that I was growing blasé and unable to enjoy things as I used. It was not until some years later that I realized there never had been any magic.

Chapter X
'Is' or 'Be'?

At the end of the dark downstairs passage of the house in Kensington Gore, near the little boxroom in which my grandfather's silk hat was kept, along with such miscellaneous objects as old riding boots, a shooting stick, pictures with broken glass and, occasionally, copies of *Punch* piled up on curtained shelves waiting eternally to be bound, was a small cloakroom. In this cloakroom there was a notice, in my grandfather's spiky, Victorian handwriting, on a postcard, yellow and curling with age, which said:

PLEASE HOLD DOWN UNTIL CISTERN BE EMPTY.

For many years those words ran through my mind in a too-familiar refrain. Constant repetition made them meaningless, until they had no more significance than the sound of train wheels on a long journey.

They were merely part of the everyday accumulation of trifles which, seen too often, seed themselves in the lower stratum of the mind without disturbing its surface and then, moved by some unaccountable force, suddenly germinate at a most unexpected time. That is why one sometimes remembers, quite suddenly and for no reason, the exact shape of a crack in one's nursery ceiling, a broken tile in the floor of a passage at school, or the pattern of a wallpaper in a long-forgotten house.

The whole business of remembering is most intricate and hard to understand. What happens to forgotten sights and experiences and do we ever really forget, or are they all put aside, suitably edited and filed by that tidy and most respectable organ, the mind, like the dusty files of *Punches* behind the curtains in the lobby at Kensington Gore, in the hope that they may be of some use at a future date? Otherwise how can it be that, though for years I could not remember what happened round the corner of a passage in my grandfather's old house on Sydenham Hill, not long ago, during a dream, I turned that corner and there it all was, just as I had last seen it twenty years ago?

I said just now that the mind was respectable. Hypocritical would be a better word, at least for the memory, and I suppose that is part of the mind. Memories are notoriously untrustworthy, not so much in what they forget but in what, after all, should be their chief function – the things they remember. Many honest, unimpeachable men have gone to their graves clearly remembering something which never happened. Take, for example, the pleasing case of the very old man who remembered actually seeing Napoleon. Scholars and historians fastened upon him like leeches. Here was an unrepeatable opportunity to discover some new fact, some hitherto unrecorded personal idiosyncrasy that might throw an entirely new light on the whole of his character. The tone of his voice, his movements, anything that had the touch of actuality. But all the old chap could remember was that the Emperor seemed to be a fine upstanding man with a long white beard. No doubt he saw Napoleon all right, and not somebody else, but he, alone among men, encumbered with his ridiculous memories, knew nothing about his appearance at all. All of which is a long way from the notice in my grandfather's downstairs cloakroom. For years, then, those few simple words ran through my head unheeded and uncriticized, as familiar as the tune of the National Anthem:

PLEASE HOLD DOWN UNTIL CISTERN BE EMPTY.

I must have read it more than three hundred and sixty-five times in a year without thinking about it. (One day a more delicate pen than mine may write a whole volume of reminiscence about these small but important apartments which play such an unchronicled part in our lives. Casting one's mind back, what a wealth of variety they represent, each with its own peculiarities. And the essential feature, the plumbing – what a reflection of the artistic and cultural tastes of the various periods it shows! 'A Hundred Years of Plumbing' – an irresistible title. And the keen student would have a reflective feast in those glazed names alone. The whole history of the last century of our race might be written round them, starting with 'The Grosvenor', in Old English Gothic lettering, and concluding with 'The Civic', in plain Roman with no serifs.)

For a large part of my childhood I had been dimly aware of that card, yellowing and faded with the afternoon sunlight which, in summertime, fell across it. Then one day, owing to one of those minor and unrecorded upheavals of the mind that mark one's growth just as surely as the pencillings on the edge of the nursery door, I read the words with a new, a seeing and a critical eye.

PLEASE HOLD DOWN UNTIL CISTERN BE EMPTY.

Why not, I thought for the first time in all those years:

PLEASE HOLD DOWN UNTIL CISTERN *IS* EMPTY?

Was it more correct to say 'be empty' than 'is empty'? If so, I realized with horror that I had been wrong all my life. I had gone about the world unknowingly making this mistake, which must have been obvious to everyone but myself. It was like those humiliating mispronunciations of adolescence – 'Pene-lowp' for Penelope, 'negotate' for negotiate – or the childish nightmare of being left, the only one in church kneeling, when everybody else has stood up. My whole previous life was shown up in a new light. I saw myself walking through the world in ignorance saying 'is empty' when everybody behind my back was smiling and excusing my gauche mistake.

That was my first reaction. Then came doubt of my grand-father himself. Up to now I had looked upon him with the uncritical eye of childhood as being infallible. (What a great deal of trouble would be saved in the world if we could only convince children that we are generally wrong and that most of the information we give them is inaccurate. It is impossible not to teach children. Every time we open our mouths in their presence we teach them something, whether we like it or not, and a good 90 per cent of what we teach them is bigoted, biased and misleading, or else purely misinformed. It is a solemn thought. Even now, owing to some quite uncon-sidered remark made in front of me when I was a child, I measure a hundred yards in my mind's eye by the distance from the front gate of the house we were living in at the time to the pillar box at the end of the road, and a mile from our house to the railway station. I know quite well they are wrong, but it is too late now. I cannot unlearn what I learned as a child.) 'Perhaps,' I thought, 'it is he who is wrong after all.' And with the first crack of doubt the whole precarious struc-ture of confidence collapsed.

No doubt there comes a time when we are ripe for dis-illusionment and this syntactical problem was rather an instrument than a cause of any change of outlook. It did not occur to me that perhaps my grandfather himself, writing the notice at his study desk years before, may have been troubled with the same doubts about his correctness, or that he might have scribbled 'is' on the blotting paper and glanced at it side-ways to see what it looked like. Still less did it occur to me that both 'is' and 'be' might be right; that in nine cases out of ten there is no unassailable right and wrong, no utter black or blank white.

No, either I or my grandfather was wrong. And with my grandfather I began to identify the whole adult world, all that I had accepted so unquestioningly hitherto. The last remnants of a comfortable reliance on face values went and I began to look about for further signs of this conspiracy to deceive and impose upon the credulity of the young.

A casual glance when my mind happened to be in a particularly critical mood had opened the flood gates of doubt. There the little card still remained, yellow and curling with its rusty drawing pin at the top, unchallenged except by myself. I alone in a condoning and hypocritical world.

PLEASE HOLD DOWN UNTIL CISTERN BE EMPTY.

My eyes were open to the world, to its deceptions and its fallibilities at last.

Chapter XI
The Swan of Bayswater

Sometimes in the evening, when my grandfather had been to the Petty Sessions, where he sat as a magistrate, he would bring home with him a certain Mr Whatley, who was, I think, Clerk to the Court. At least, I know that he was a gentleman of some standing in the legal world and that he has since become, not plain 'Mr Whatley', but 'Sir Wilfred'.

There would be a slight stir in the household when this tall, white-headed figure with its distinguished profile was seen getting out of the car after my grandfather. Aunt Maria would have to move her Patience from the study table to the little conservatory behind the drawing-room and Aunt Pem would also be banished upstairs in case her anxiety to please should cause her fresh paroxysms of laughter.

They made a well-contrasted pair as they walked up the few yards of tiled path from the wrought-iron gate to the front door: Mr Whatley tall, grave and white, with a swan-like poise and consciousness of his own appearance, and my grandfather, short, red and smiling, trotting beside him on his stiff little legs.

As Jonzen opened the front door, letting the roar of traffic swirl like a flood through the downstairs rooms, Aunt Pem, laughing nervously, would be scarcely round the bend of the staircase leading to the drawing-room, and the study, when my grandfather led the way into it, rubbing his hands and clicking his false teeth, would still have that slightly guilty and secretive air of a room too hurriedly and too recently evacuated. My grandfather, aware of this, would rub his hands all the harder and smile more deprecatingly in an endeavour to offset it, and Mr Whatley would raise his voice with a conscious display of good breeding and carry the conversation himself for a few minutes to put my grandfather at his ease and show that he, as a man of good family and some social standing, knew perfectly how to glide over these uneasy moments and that my grandfather, who had made his money in trade, could not be expected to handle the situation with such suavity and poise.

Occasionally, if Mr Whatley's approach was more than usually sudden and unheralded, I would find myself trapped in the dark recess of the study with no chance of escape and, after my grandfather had drawn Mr Whatley's attention to me and he had acknowledged it with a grave and stately inclination of the head, it was more prudent to remain where I was, bowed over the war numbers of *Punch* or Leech's illustrations to *Mr Sponge's Sporting Tour* in the half darkness of the inner room than to venture past the two seated figures to the hall door. I would sit there turning over the dusty pages, politely pretending to be absorbed, while my grandfather and Mr Whatley discussed the day's proceedings in Court over a whisky and soda poured generously by my grandfather and received graciously but not humbly; or while Mr Whatley recounted a personal anecdote introducing the name of some notoriety whom my grandfather could not be expected to have met. Pouring over *Mr Sponge* at the dark end of the room I would try not to overhear all that was said, but, with my attention half distracted to my book, the recurrent words 'we Whatleys' forced themselves on my mind as they flashed by with the rhythmic insistence of telegraph poles on a train journey.

In recounting these stories about his family, Mr Whatley was indulging his little weakness in a way that would not have been possible in the presence of one of his own social standing, and it was the price he asked for the honour of his presence in my grandfather's house. All this was understood and tacitly agreed upon as my grandfather sat listening attentively, with a genial smile on his face, or laughed outright, patting himself on the thigh with a stubby hand and saying: 'Capital, capital!' with the over-appreciative manner of a young schoolboy applauding an older boy and a respected ringleader of his set. My grandfather realized fully that he could not expect the patronage of one of 'we Whatleys' without some sacrifice either of dignity or sincerity, so he smiled a little more deprecatingly, laughed with a little more flattery than he actually felt. Like all self-made men whose wealth has come from commerce, my grandfather had a secret contempt for the more favoured professional classes, though he did not show it in their presence. Many, possibly including Mr Whatley himself, came under the general heading, to quote my grandfather's own words, of those who 'couldn't make a living at an apple stall'. But this was an opinion only expressed at breakfast, or on some other occasion when my grandfather was alone with his family. Whatever his secret opinion of Mr Whatley might have been, he hid it under a smiling and respectful exterior and Mr Whatley, for his part, though he might, with that glazed and uninformative eye, have been noting the mediocrity of our pictures – a photogravure of the child Handel discovered by his parents playing the spinet in a loft and another called *His First Commission*, showing a small child drawing a beautiful lady in the dress of Charles the Second, while her cavalier sweetheart looks on – did not for a moment relax his gentlemanly, even friendly manner. For, besides being an excellent listener and one on whom he could safely inflict his little weakness, my grandfather was many times richer than he, though, of course, it was the process of amassing that fortune and the source from which it came that formed the unbridgable gulf between them. On the whole, then, the balance was finely adjusted and each contrived, with a delicate nicety, to keep it so.

However long they chose to sit on, my grandfather with his short legs stretched out on his hassock and Mr Whatley with his fine, swan-like profile turned towards me, talking, smiling, nodding their acquiescence – Mr Whatley to my grandfather's wealth, my grandfather to Mr Whatley's breeding and position – it would not be possible or correct to disturb them. As dinnertime drew near Jonzen would bustle in and out of the study on the most flimsy pretext, breathing ponderously and hoping, by the frequency of her interruptions, to dislodge them. At last Mr Whatley would rise and say that he was keeping us from our dinner, and my grandfather, with many polite protestations, would see him to the front door. There would be a sudden gush of sound again as the traffic noise washed and swirled round the passages, a few words of parting on the doorstep – my grandfather warmly and affably inviting Mr Whatley to call in again another evening and Mr Whatley assuring him with impeccable politeness that nothing would please him more – then the heavy front door would bang to and once more I would have that feeling of security, of remoteness from the cold, unfriendly world of rushing taxis and limousines, of pale and unassailable Mr Whatleys.

As soon as the door was closed the house would revert to its old genial simplicity. Jonzen would announce: 'Dinner is sairved', Aunt Pem and Aunt Maria would return from the drawing-room and my grandmother would appear from nowhere in particular, for she had a talent for disappearing apparently from the face of the earth when somebody came whom she did not like, and she did not like Mr Whatley.

The house returned to its old simplicity, but it was not quite the same, at any rate to me, for Mr Whatley seemed to linger behind like a chill breath from the outer world. For the first time I noticed that the furniture was extremely old-fashioned and rather tasteless, that Jonzen, as she breathed heavily in the background behind the dining-table, should have been a butler. Mr Whatley seemed to leave behind him a sneer as impalpable but unmistakable as the Cheshire Cat's grin.

The sneer would hang on the air of the dining-room all through dinner. My grandfather, realizing that Mr Whatley was not popular in the household, became half shamefaced and half resentful, while my grandmother made it as plain as possible that she did not approve of his friend by apologizing to everyone that the dinner was over-cooked and sending a message to Ellen by Jonzen to say that she fully realized that it was not in the least her fault. Aunt Pem, dimly conscious that something was wrong but quite unable to guess what it might be, would try to put my grandfather in a good temper by saying, just as we all felt the subject could not be mentioned any more, that she thought Mr Whatley a very handsome man and that he really seemed to enjoy coming as he always stayed such a long time.

My own feeling was that, though I was slightly sorry for my grandfather, I also felt he had betrayed us all in some way; that his too subservient manner had allowed the vaguely disquieting sneer to hang behind, like cigar smoke, round the curtains, the pictures and in the upholstery of the chairs. It had been a shock to see him off his guard, so overawed. Before it had always been he who was grand and awe-inspiring. We, as members of his family, had allowed ourselves willingly to be dominated by him. If he said there were to be oysters on Wednesdays there were oysters; if, when somebody was threatened by a wasp, he announced in the solemn tones of a judge pronouncing sentence: 'Death seldom ensues', then we were subdued. Now he had sold us all merely for the momentary goodwill of a well-bred but supercilious swan.

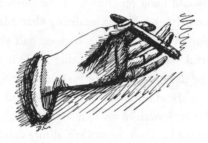

Chapter XII
The Dog's-eye View

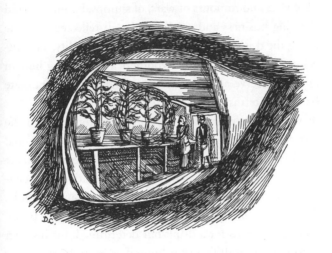

Sometimes it seems that only the tremendous is worth writing about, that everything one reads or writes should be full of mighty catastrophes or upheavals and that nothing less is worthwhile. Earthquakes, wars, tragedies and triumphs have stretched our compass to such an extent that the sheer ordinariness of ordinary people and their lives seems absurdly trivial by comparison. But there is a virtue in triviality. I remember looking into a dog's eye when I was a child and being surprised to see reflected, not only myself, but the whole garden. There it all was, complete and exact, in brilliant miniature.

To the truly discriminating human being, if there ever is one, the slightest, most unconsidered action – the striking of a match or a sudden laugh – can be as significant as all the discoveries of science during a lifetime. There it is, the whole world of wars and rumours of wars, of slumps, booms, art and religion, big business and small minds, all reflected, like the garden in the dog's eye, by some unnoticed triviality. The difficult but pleasant task of the hypothetical discerning human being is to observe and decode these trivialities, to translate the banal into terms of the eternal.

Therefore, as my grandfather strutted stiffly across to the farthest corner of the room to pour out his whisky and soda, I should, with my dog's eye, have been able to reconstruct from it the whole intricate business of civilization. For civilization is organized self-discipline and civilization as a whole, I feel, could not be better expressed than by the figure of my grandfather, anxious for a drink but determined, for his own good, to make it as difficult for himself as possible, stumping across the room whistling 'O Rest in the Lord' under his breath and then, when his self-imposed difficulties were overcome, pouring himself out an extra large one.

The real adventures and experiences, then, are small and often unnoticed. In fact, the greatest adventures of all are those of the mind, that happen within ourselves, and the real adventurers are those who can wring experience even from waiting on a railway station, while others may travel round the world or jump out of aeroplanes daily and remain just the same. The Chinese, those masters of harnessing the ordinary, make miniature gardens with dwarf trees, as perfect and as satisfying to the cultured eye as an estate, and all in a space no larger than a tea tray.

Carrying this theory to its full extent one might argue that it should not be necessary to travel when one can 'see the world in a handful of dust'. Didn't I see and experience years ago, as I followed my grandmother round the long green-houses at Sydenham Hill, the whole of the tropics in miniature, condensed to the size of a glasshouse? (And, after all, what is mere size? Would Botticelli's *Birth of Venus* be any better for being fifty times as big, or Bach's *St Matthew Passion* a hundred times as long?) Now, whenever I smell geraniums, especially in conjunction with blistered hot-water pipes, I am back once more on a Saturday morning following my grandmother down the long perspective of the greenhouse with Ray, the gardener. I am poking idly at the plants, picking the paint blisters in the humid, over-scented atmosphere. Supposing then, after all the trouble and expense of a journey to the tropics, I should find myself, like Alice and the Red Queen, back where I started so long ago on Sydenham Hill?

It is much the same in the sphere of mental adventure and experience. If my grandfather did not actually commit murder there was murder in his eye as it followed a wasp round the breakfast table and into the marmalade pot and then, as he leant slowly towards it, '*The Times* Newspaper' in one hand and a knife in the other, before squashing, crunching and annihilating it over the tablecloth with all the strength in his body. It was a dog's-eye tragedy – for the wasp – and, for the time being, my grandfather was a murderer in miniature.

Life at Kensington was placid and uneventful. It went by in

a series of days smoothly alike with no melodrama greater than the killing of a wasp, the sudden slamming of a door or, perhaps, somebody whistling in the street at night, but it was none the less life.

Chapter XIII
Upstairs, Downstairs

In the morning, when my grandfather was due to leave for the office, there was always a sharp encounter between Lucy and Jonzen for the honour of putting on his coat. Sometimes Ellen also would take part. Five minutes before the appointed time the hall would be completely empty, with my grandfather's gloves and bowler hat waiting on the table. As soon as he approached, with *The Times* in one hand and his slip-on glasses in the other, humming to himself and trying to look unconscious of the impending scene, Lucy and Jonzen somehow were there, waiting for him. (They seemed to have the same miraculous powers of manifestation as the ticket collectors in Kensington Gardens. One only has to sit down in an apparently deserted part to find a collector at one's elbow immediately. Many times I have tried to discover how this trick was done and sat deliberately, trying to look in all directions at once, only to hear behind me that deprecating cough and the preparatory ting of the ticket punch. I am forced to the conclusion that, through working for so long on Peter Pan's home ground, they have learned the secret of invisibility. Either that or else the London County Council allows them to live in hollow trees.) Every day the same scene took place. One or other of them would seize his overcoat while the remaining one hovered round, not daring actually to interfere, but determined to make things as difficult as possible for the victor. Between them my grandfather would be pushed this way and that, brushed, patted, shaken and, if Jonzen happened to be successful, pulled right up on tiptoe as he put his arms into his overcoat, for she was a powerful woman, a good head taller than my grandfather, and in the excitement of the moment she frequently forgot her strength.

My grandfather's attitude throughout the whole affair was passive. It was never his habit to question anybody about their job and the daily battle, though it made him feel slightly awkward as the two women fussed about him, tugged down his coat and picked imaginary pieces of fluff from his collar, was all due entirely to excessive zeal. He did not interfere in household questions beyond examining the tradesmen's books at the end of the week and glancing over the list of expenses in connection with the car which Parsons always prepared, and I do not remember that he ever questioned anything, for when he did trust anyone – and he trusted everyone whose hair was not red – he did so blindly.

Lucy had been in my grandfather's household forty years and Ellen the same. There was no life to Lucy other than that of my grandfather's family and descendants, except for 'me sisters' – 'me sister Rose', 'me sister Alice', 'me sister Cassie', 'me sister Sarah' and 'me sister Lottie'. Perhaps in a few generations' time the whole relationship of servant and employer will seem fantastic and absurd. It may be hard to convince anyone that human beings can live together in the same house for years without really knowing one another and without ever saying exactly what they mean. But to our generation the whole careful relationship of deceit and artificiality, of partial kindness and generosity on the one side and of partial devotion on the other seems so natural as to be almost unnoticed. It seemed quite normal to us that as soon as the door was closed behind them – or even before – we should repeat stories of their amusing mispronunciations ('Good enough for *Punch,* my dear!'), while we knew quite well that downstairs they were laughing at us and probably entertaining their friends at our expense. There is a pleasing element of mutual hypocrisy which, I fancy, will be a rich source of research for future sociologists.

In the elaborate hierarchy of the kitchen and servants' quarters Lucy stood high, as she had been with my grandfather so long. It was really right, then, that she should have helped him on with his coat in the mornings, but then the front door was Jonzen's job, being parlourmaid. So a delicate situation was created which my grandfather, looking rather shamefaced in the midst of this too feminine display of devotion, did not attempt to solve. When he had gone and the front door had slammed to, Lucy would hobble back upstairs to her sewing-room, her face contorted with anxiety – for what nobody could imagine.

It seems that worry and anxiety are necessary constituents of the human mind. If there is nothing reasonable to worry about a cause must be invented. How much more sensible and rational are animals with their so-called lower intelligence. One never sees a dog or cat racked with worry or an anxious expression on the face of a cow. They know quite well that somebody else has the unenviable job of feeding them. Their subsistence is assured, so why should they worry?

Lucy's position was just as secure, yet she was forced to create imaginary dangers to balance her mental diet. Years before, when my grandfather's family were children, she made them fold their clothes neatly every night by saying: 'Supposing the house was to catch fire, you wouldn't want the firemen to see your clothes put away all any'ow.' No domestic animal, relieved of the necessity to struggle for its livelihood, could have achieved such a high degree of imaginative anxiety.

Writing letters was to Lucy what a sewing-machine is to a canary. As soon as she saw my mother writing at the study desk she would hover in the background, pick up the copper ashtray with the profile of Mr Winkle in the bottom, polish it on her apron and put it down again automatically, without knowing what she was doing, then she would say: 'Well, ma dear, I don't want to worry you, but . . .' and the unquenchable flow would begin. Perhaps it would be whether or not to light the drawing-room fire or which of the 'young girls' was to have a half day, or perhaps about Jonzen, who had a habit of 'slipping into a little crêpe de Chine and going out to get some fresh air in her lungs' at unspecified moments, or perhaps the deeper and more far-reaching problem of spring cleaning. 'Well, ma dear, I told yer puppa, I said: "If I was you," I said, "I should only 'ave the front rooms done this year because if you ask me the 'ole of the back of the 'ouse is going to fall out." But there, it doesn't do to look on the gloomy side, does it? Well, as you know, I always was one to see the funny side meself. Many's the time I've said to old Ellen: "Well, Ellen," I've said, "I wish someone'd give me a good 'it down the spine to make me laugh."' And she would pause a moment to straighten the ornaments on the mantelpiece – tiny brass figures of Sam Weller and Sairy Gamp which, no doubt, caused Mr Whatley an inward smile. 'But there, it isn't for me to say which rooms 'e 'as done, of course. It's just as 'e says, but . . .' flicking abstractedly with a duster. 'Of course I don't want you to think I mind the work. It's not that at all. Well, no one can't say that I was ever one for getting out of the work. Old Ellen, she was always one for a lark. "Come on, Luce, you're only young once," she used to say, but I was never so 'appy as when I 'ad somethink to polish. Well, I always did say that the 'appiest 'oliday I ever spent was that time yer mother took the little 'ouse at Woolacombe and I 'ad Master Reggie, Miss Marjory and Miss Winnie down with scarlet fever. Oh, Master Reggie, 'e was a little terror. The things 'e used to get up to – well there. I couldn't 'elp but laugh, 'e was that comical. Yer mother always used to say: "Well, Lucy, you 've got patience," but then I was never one to mind what the children did, as you know. Of course, it's not like that now, with these "young girls". Not that little Ivy isn't quite a good little thing in some ways, but it isn't like it was with the "young girls" as I always told yer mother. I told her it's not as though you can say: "You do sech a thing and I'll put up the curtains" like, if you see what I mean. I 'ope you don't think I'm grumbling, ma dear, because, as you know, I never was one to grumble. I don't even mind doing the grates and that, though I never 'ave been used to doing the fires. As you know, I never was one to mind what I do, but it's just that come the winter it's the dark mornings.'

And as my mother retreated up the stairs to the drawing-room she would hear Lucy's voice trailing on to nobody in the study, rising occasionally to shrill vehemence, then lapsing back to a steady reminiscent drone. It did not really matter to her that nobody was listening. Like a true artist she did not depend on an audience. It was art for art's sake. Long after my mother was settled at the desk by the drawing-room window she could hear, far away below, Lucy still talking to no one in an empty room.

The whole relationship of employer and employee was delicate and strange; an elaborate compound of condescension on the one hand and servility on the other. In former days a vast, anonymous army of piano tuners, french polishers and clock-winders crept noiselessly and subserviently in and out of the houses of the well-to-do, moving with the practised silence of a lifetime spent in making themselves as nearly invisible as the too solid flesh of humanity would allow. How many times in our youth have we not heard those odd, unrhythmic notes coming from an apparently deserted drawing-room – an unearthly, mournful noise like the tapping of a lost spirit, as perhaps it was – and been told not to go in because the piano tuner was there? But apart from a strange bowler hat on the hall chair – a bowler hat at once so meek and respectable that it seemed to be saying 'Excuse me, sir' every time one looked at it – and perhaps a grey wraith flitting noiselessly to the front door, there was no actual manifestation of the piano tuner himself. One did not know his name, his religion, his politics or even his size in boots.

This semi-abolition of the physical presence had its drawbacks. When my mother and her sisters were children it was a recognized fact that as soon as the conversation had taken a more than usually ridiculous turn there would be a slight rustling, a gentle cough and the clock man would be among them, shrinking himself into the smallest possible space and trying his hardest to look as though he did not possess the sense of sound, sight or speech. No doubt they felt genuinely sorry for him and may even have said: 'Good morning', but it must have been sad to go through life knowing that, as one entered a room, laughter would be smothered and that, before the door was closed behind one, it would burst out again twice as loudly.

Chapter XIV
The Pleasures of Prejudice

My grandfather, as I have said, was an exceptionally easy-going man. I seldom heard him utter a word of condemnation and never remember having seen him really angry. The worst that his children ever had to fear from him was that he would call one of them a 'little goose', that was the extent of his awfulness, and this happened so seldom that, when it did, the effect was all the more powerful.

He had, however, some very fine prejudices apart from red-haired men and boots with toe-caps. One of the best of these was against long telephone conversations. If one of us spoke for more than a few minutes he would lower his *Times* and say with unshakable authority: 'The telephone was not made for private conversation,' as though he had it from the lips of Mr Edison himself.

Perhaps this was due partly to the fact that he took to the telephone late in life. He would only use it reluctantly and when he did he would speak with that insulting loudness and clarity that English travellers of the past used when addressing foreigners and, to the last, he opened all telephone conversations with the archaic formula: 'Are you there?'

There were many human frailties which my grandfather could pass over with scarcely a frown. In most respects he was exceptionally liberal and humane in his point of view. Drunkenness he accepted, as all lovers of Mr Pickwick necessarily must, as inevitable – at least in others. He would merely quote an old veterinary friend of his youth who advised him: 'Never get drunk before breakfast, Mr Richard,' and leave it at that. All the conventional forms of domestic immorality were so far removed from him that he never even bothered to pass judgement on them. In short, he was the last person to be carping and censorious, but toe-caps or a telephone conversation that was not brutally curt and concise were more than he could bear. All his rational tolerance would disappear at once. 'The telephone was not made for private conversation.' He spoke with extreme authority because he spoke from prejudice and not from reason.

There is a primitive pleasure in abandoning one's intelligence and giving way to a good prejudice that is like lying back in a bath that one knows to be too hot. From my earliest youth I disliked all children called Ernest. There has never been the slightest reason for this. I was never, to my know-ledge, slighted in the cradle by an Ernest. No, my dislike is founded on something far deeper and more lasting than mere reason. (Ernest! There is something furtive, something pale and malignant about the sound of the word.) The amount of harmless pleasure I've had from disliking the name Ernest is incalculable. I only hope that I may never meet an Ernest who disproves my prejudice, or an unlimited joy will be denied me.

I have also derived considerable quiet satisfaction from dis-liking rhododendrons, pine trees and all the other products of a sandy soil. There may be parts of Surrey and Hampshire – large stretches in the direction of the New Forest – which are both sandy and beautiful, but nothing would induce me to admit it.

Strongly entrenched in my prejudice, impregnably fortified by stupidity, I will not see beauty where there is sand. In a uni-verse shattered with doubts, full of faiths that I would give much to believe in with all my heart, I am completely certain of only two things: that the name Ernest is evil and that there can be no beauty on a sandy soil.

I am certain of these things because I am prejudiced, there-fore ignorant about them. For certainty comes only from ignorance, not knowledge, and the most self-confident men are the most stupid. Their confidence is merely a prejudice in their own favour. It comes from that most priceless asset which a benign Providence can bestow – an inability to see any other side to an argument but one's own. Without this inestimable quality no man can rise to greatness in this world. Where there is division or doubt in the mind there is weakness and where there is weakness there can be no authority. Men of authority, I maintain, all have this one quality in common – a great, a shining and an imperishable stupidity. That is, men who truly believe in their authority, who do not know in secret that they are wrong most of the time and who do not wield their authority for its own sake but because they know it to be a necessity, and with the tongue at least partly in the cheek.

Authority itself is irrational. Dr Johnson's Latin master beat him for not being able to answer the most abstruse questions. As Johnson said, if he had been able to answer them he would never have gone to school, but all the same he was the first to admit that he owed most of his exceptional knowledge of the classics to this tyrannical man.

Only the luxuriously bigoted, wallowing in the bath of prejudice and turning on the hot tap, really believe that black is black and white is white, he is wrong and I am right. They must be happily ignorant of nine-tenths of the world and – still greater blessing – totally ignorant of themselves. 'Where ignorance is bliss', etc. etc. Turn on the hot tap. Let the steam swirl. Lie back and close the eyes. Blessed are the bigoted, for they shall have peace of mind.

Chapter XV
A Puff of Cigar Smoke

History, both personal and universal, could be admirably recorded in smells, if there were any way of perpetuating them. (What a pleasant and instructive record it would be, and what a chance for that neglected, unappreciated organ, the nose!) All that could be said about my grandfather in the space of twenty books could be summed up instantly in one whiff of cigar smoke. It is like the entry of the Demon King in pantomime: a puff of smoke, and out of it comes, not horns and a tail, for nothing could be less demoniacal than my grandfather, especially after dinner, but a round smiling figure with the childlike look of an Edward Lear drawing.

There is a period flavour in cigar smoke reminiscent of distant days of sybaritic ease – like mental waistcoat buttons bursting – that belies my grandfather, for he never smoked more than two cigars a day. He was rigid about this, just as he was rigid about getting up at half-past seven in the morning, having a cold bath – with or without a purple bath mat – and riding with his friends in the Row. Though he enjoyed making money – and there is no doubt that he did immensely enjoy it for its own sake – he also took great pleasure in living far below his income. Indulgence, to him, was even more exquisite when it was curbed and disciplined. That is why he made himself walk from one end of the room to the other for his nightly whisky. To have had it beside him would have been cheating. It would have been short-circuiting the law on which his whole life had been founded: the law of overcoming obstacles. He knew that the whole secret of value is in rarity, so he rarely allowed himself pleasures and when he did they were all the more pleasant.

Cigar smoke and the sound of horses' hoofs, how unfailingly they evoke the sight of my grandfather returning from the office in a phaeton driven by old Bob Smith! Already my grandfather, who one felt would certainly live for ever, a symbol of immortality, seems to have sunk into the improbable past. Then one whiff of cigar smoke – something happens inside the nose, messages are sent hurriedly to the brain. There is a consultation. Mental archives are searched, files are examined under the letter H for 'hands (gouty)' and C for 'countenance (red)'. My grandfather always used the word 'countenance' instead of 'face'. All women, or nearly all, he would admit to be beautiful, pretty or, at the least, pleasing, but the most he would say of any man was that he had a 'nice open countenance'. Then, in the space of a hundredth part of a second or so, I am back in the house in Kensington Gore with the study fire leaping and the curtains drawn. My grandfather is squinting down his nose, in his armchair by the smoking table, to see whether his cigar is properly alight; there are two new books from Mudie's Library on the table with the evening paper; Jonzen has just gone out of the door into her pantry breathing heavily and, in some odd way, I feel, disapprovingly as though she had a grievance; and we are in for another evening of the indecipherable *Fortunes of Nigel.*

With the smell still in my nose I can remember what I had forgotten for many years; that, though they were happy evenings and I had nothing but respect and affection for my grandfather, Nigel and his fortunes brought a feeling of frustration, almost of claustrophobia. The evening paper was there on the table. I could see it out of the corner of my eye. I longed to emerge from Nigel's world of dusty verbosity into the comparative reality of journalism. It would have been like coming out of a long tunnel into sudden daylight. And it was not only Nigel. That smell of cigar smoke also reminds me that, happy though it was, it was a period of suppression and insincerity. There were many tastes and opinions to be suppressed and held, passionately, in secret. For, though I rebelled against Nigel and all he stood for in art, literature, music and politics, I had not the moral courage to say so openly in the face of overwhelming opposition, and continued to express admiration where I did not feel it and pretended to views which I had long since ceased to hold. At the age of seventeen I felt myself to be leading a double life. There I sat, after a good dinner, in front of the study fire about to read, with apparent pleasure, the novels of Scott, whom I detested and, in my lofty adolescence, despised heartily, while all the time I was a secret radical, heretic and unbeliever. Because my opinions were held in secret they were all the more dear to me. I was like an early Christian in a heathen land, I felt, as I sat pretending to enjoy Scott and Dickens by my grandfather's fireside, burning – ungratefully, as it now seems – with a fierce, disruptive light within.

Jonzen comes in with another scuttleful of coal, breathing more heavily and more disapprovingly than ever. It is going to be a warm, cosy evening in the study at Kensington. My grandfather draws hard at his cigar once or twice. Then takes it out to see how it is burning. Satisfied that it is well alight he sits back and expands into a smile. There is a short pause while he abandons himself to the first ambrosial puffs. The fire leaps and dances. Traffic in the street, somewhere beyond the heavy curtains of the study window, rumbles by with a steady, deadened roar which accentuates the feeling of well-fed security inside my grandfather's study. Outside in London it is theatre time. Lighted buses hurry along Kensington Gore towards the West End, each a cosmos in itself. Taxis whisk the furred and bejewelled from the immunity of their own doorsteps into the stream. The dim-lit pavements are full of disembodied footsteps. In the half light every girl seems unbelievably beautiful. Typists who, in the cruel reality of morning, are plain and unnoticeable, are now, as they trip along by the Park railings or wait in dark clusters at the bus stops, all as promising of perfection as the veiled beauties of the East. Theatreland is brilliant. The taxis which swooped to the pavement in Pont Street, Queen's Gate and Prince's Gardens unload their gorgeous passengers and slide away into oblivion. Pit queues are beginning to shuffle forward hopefully while the street entertainers rush through the last part of their performance with one eye on the street corner. Everywhere there is bustling chaos and an undercurrent of Rabelaisian vitality. The population of London has changed completely; the whole tempo has accelerated. The door of a saloon bar opens and a man comes out, shouts something back over his shoulder, there is a roar of laughter and a glimpse of a smoking, beer-smelling crush. The door slams to. The man stops, spits and goes off still grinning at his own cleverness. It is quiet in the Park. Hunched figures stand pressed together in the darkness while the passer-by tries hard to pretend that they do not exist. It looks a miserable business, this speechless love-making in dark archways and on park benches. The passer-by hurries on apologetically to his family and fireside with a feeling partly of sympathy and partly of self-righteousness. He hurries on into the little pool of lamplight, then on into darkness once more, past the next seat with its single figure, dark and still in the half light. White legs and a white face, shadowed eye sockets that might be looking at one or might not.

My grandfather blows out a long breath and the smoke coils and eddies up towards the inverted electric light bowl in the centre of the room, where a frenzied fly is buzzing madly to and fro trying to get out. 'Well, my boy,' my grandfather says at last, 'where did we leave our friend Nigel last night? He'd just met old Sir Mungo Malagrowther, if I remember rightly.' The buses outside stop at the pavement opposite, pick up their loads and groan on. The evening paper lies on top of the library books unread. I go over to the heavy old bookcase and draw *The Fortunes of Nigel* from its place in the standard edition of the Waverley Novels and my grandfather, beaming all over his kindly face, settles himself down for the evening.

Chapter XVI
A Rearguard Action

All through my childhood the possibility that my grandfather would not live for ever did not enter my head. It was not to be contemplated that there could be an existence without either the house on Sydenham Hill or the one at Kensington Gore. It was impossible also to imagine a life without, somewhere in the background, that solid and reassuring mass of wealth and prestige, never publicly mentioned but as essential to the conditioning of our private universe as the law of gravity itself.

After all, he behaved as though he intended to live for ever, in spite of his breakfast-time recital of obituaries and fatal accidents which seemed to bring him such comfort. Those daily habits, the temperate restrictions on smoking or drinking by daytime; all carefully planned and rigidly executed, set in motion a rhythmical process which my grandfather himself would have been powerless to stop. Indeed, it sometimes seemed as though these habits became too much for him, as though they bore him along at a pace livelier than that of his own choosing, like a man on a bicycle with no brakes when he comes unexpectedly to a steep hill. He was in a dilemma. Jealous of his reputation as a Remarkable Old Man, he continued with his hunting and his awe-inspiring ablutions, but in doing so he ran the risk of killing himself and thus spoiling his record.

For many years, indulging his preference for all kinds of frugality, he went to his office by bus. He would leave the house at the same moment every morning and plunge, one felt, spiritually naked into the rapids of London's work-going traffic – or if not naked, then clothed only in a sense of self-preservation tuned to hansom cabs and horse-drawn buses. After many perilous moments in which my grandfather, slightly bewildered and clutching his bowler hat to his head, seemed to be buffeted hither and thither like a cork in the lethal stream, he would reach the bus stop on the other side and, boarding a number 46 or 52, not only would he climb to the top out of bravado, but make his way down the lurching aisle to the very front seat. There, as he was borne away out of sight towards Knightsbridge, we could see him settle down with a look of satisfaction on his face, waiting for the supreme moment when the conductor came to collect his fare – for he had a free pass.

Then, as he approached his eightieth year, the brakeless

bicycle he had made for himself began to gather speed and my grandfather, still committed to his spartan way of living, came gradually to realize in his heart that the pace was too much for him. The realization came, I think, very slowly and he fought it back hour by hour, knowing that once the careful routine was broken he would be abandoned to old age. (That is the disadvantage of a carefully planned, abstemious and hard-working life. In the end the abstemious worker is in the same predicament as the habitual drunkard. Deny one his bottle and the other his office desk or his cold bath and each is reduced to ruin. The inference is obvious. Work, when indulged to excess, is just as much of a vice in the eyes of an all-seeing Nature as dipsomania.) He became pathetically glad of an excuse not to have his cold bath, he was troubled by a mysterious stiffness in arms and legs and a persistent cough. Though he struggled tenaciously he was forced to give ground week by week, month by month, with the certain knowledge that each inch yielded could never be regained.

He began going to doctors. One very distinguished specialist, a riding acquaintance, whom he consulted about his cough, merely told him that at his age he was lucky to be able to cough at all – and charged him five guineas. He went through all the stages of self-delusion and hope, of secret and unexpressed disappointments, of new cures that were to succeed where all else had failed but which, after a day or two, were tactfully not mentioned again. Still he continued to grow more and more lame. Then, with the pioneering spirit which persuaded him to open the marmalade pot after so many years, he tried osteopathy. Whether it was the stimulus of trying something new I do not know, but at any rate a battle was won in his perpetual rearguard action against old age, a valuable amount of time gained. He resumed his early morning rides, his old Pickwickian *joie de vivre*, and even, when no adequate excuse could be found to relieve him, the detestable cold bath. Wednesday evenings saw him once more in the blue-spotted waistcoat, with a dozen oysters before him and a glass of sherry wine at his side. Summer evenings were once again spent trotting round the solemn, sunlit galleries of Burlington House with his marked catalogue open in his hand and the slip-on glasses ready if he should want to peer closely at a particular piece of brushwork or a signature; or else dozed away in the no less solemn precincts of the Oval, in the shadow of those venerated gasometers, watching Hobbs make one of his quiet, gentlemanly centuries.

It was a brief Indian Summer and I think he knew it as he sat on the hard benches of the Members' Stand or paused on one of the hot gratings in Burlington House to admire once more a particular favourite. The inevitable conclusion could not be long delayed, so he made the most of each day and crowded as much happy, unsensational living as he could into it. Before very long, he knew, his own obituary notice would be read out, to mingle with the crunching of toast at many other breakfast tables.

Chapter XVII
Derby Day 1928

In the beginning of his seventy-eighth year my grandfather went for a cruise in the Mediterranean where he picked up a germ and developed a bad fever. As soon as he arrived home he went to bed. But he was obviously very ill and within a week or ten days he was dead. At the time Lucy blamed herself entirely for not packing his thicker pants, as though, deterred by the extra wool, the germ might have turned back.

It was always rather a grief to me that a man so deeply and essentially English, so representative of much, both good and less good, in the England of his time, should have fallen a victim to a foreign germ. One felt that, with his almost naïve insularity, he must have been as defenceless against continental diseases as he was baffled by continental pronunciation. One felt also that he was well fortified to resist all upright, above-board English ailments, such as gout or high blood pressure, but that this was a mean and treacherous attack from an unexpected quarter.

Apart from this there was much that was strangely appropriate in his death, for it was Derby Day and he had been to something like fifty Derbys, rattling through south London and over Epsom Downs in the coach-and-four which belonged to the business. Also it was seven-thirty in the morning, the exact moment when the little knot of friends was collecting round the mounting block in the Gardens opposite. It was a fine morning in early summer – and Derby Day. (It was also, rather unfortunately for my grandfather, the fourth of June, so that those members of the medical profession who were not at Epsom were at Eton.) If my grandfather was killed by a foreign germ, he chose to die on the most typically English day in all the year. My grandmother might have said that it was selfish of him to die just when he knew that everybody wanted to go to the Derby, but I think it was a last gesture of defiance – it was the same spirit of petulance that caused him, on the mornings when he had written her the household cheque, to leave my grandmother at the front door without turning round or even raising his hat. Perhaps it was also the same streak of hardness as that which caused him to read out, every Christmas, on the morning of the day when he had promised to take his family to the pantomime: 'We are very sorry to state that Aladdin has been taken ill and will not be able to appear this afternoon,' and then to watch the look of dismay and disappointment cross the faces of his children.

The junk in the boxroom has been sifted through; all the dust sheets thrown back and their muddled, inconsequent treasures examined. My grandfather at the window acknowledging the salute of the passing coach with a flourish of his cigar – a glitter of bright paint, a flash and clatter of brass in the afternoon sunlight and the vision is gone with a rhythm of hoofs and a rumble of wheels that carry it away round the curve in time, towards Kensington Palace and eternity, and leaves Aunt Pem, a disembodied smile, still following it with her eyes from the long drawing-room window.

Pull back another sheet and there is my grandfather setting out across Kensington Gardens in the gathering gloom, drawn by the invisible force which compelled him, as soon as he knew it was closing time, to cross the Gardens alone, like a rowing boat on the Atlantic, while the handbells tolled, keepers' voices wailed like spirits through the trees and lights in neighbouring buildings or buses outside the railings snapped on one by one.

Or perhaps it is Sunday afternoon and we are expecting some of his riding friends to tea. The drawing-room fire is alight, though it is really not needed. The drawing-room fire is Jonzen's job and her heavy breathing, as she brings in the silver teapot and cake stand, shows, in the telepathic manner of servants, that she did not intend to have to lay it again this season. We stand at the drawing-room windows in our best clothes, watching the top of Queen's Gate if it is to be Mr Meadows, the good-natured, jovial banking friend who, like my grandfather, still wears the top hat and morning coat of a vanished era. Or if it is to be the two Miss Andersons from Bayswater, who tell such delightfully amusing stories without a smile, but with hats that nod knowingly when the point is reached, then we shall be looking in the other direction, down the gardens towards the Albert Memorial, where a few decorous promenaders are examining the first crocuses, pausing a moment in the sun.

Under another sheet are the carved wood smoking table and the old blue-spotted waistcoat, mute reminders of my grandfather at ease, of Jorrocks, Pickwick, and My Uncle Toby, of winter nights with the curtains drawn, of '*The Times* Newspaper' and 'sherry wine'. They are somehow romantic, and at the same time a trifle pathetic now, like the stage properties of some long-disbanded theatrical company – shabby, but still with a faint whiff of faded glamour about them.

Lot four, ladies and gentlemen: one grey bowler hat, worn by my grandfather at the Van Horse Parade, held at the Royal Botanical Gardens, Regent's Park and, occasionally, when my grandmother insisted that he should go, to the gardens of Chelsea Hospital for the Flower Show. Also one catalogue of the Summer Exhibition of the Royal Academy, for the year 1927, heavily marked at all pleasantly seductive landscapes, with a preference for racehorses or roses, or at all portraits of particularly beautiful and virtuous-looking women – and a membership ticket for the Oval, much thumbed, of the same date.

The dust sheets are all back in place once more, the remnants of my grandfather, a little decayed here and faded there, a little frayed by forgetfulness and nibbled by time, are reinterred. The heavy front door has closed for the last time, shutting out the rumbling traffic and the superciliousness of the swan-like Mr Whatley, Jonzen has heaved her last gusty sigh of complaint and the last cold bath has gurgled down the waste-pipe into the bowels of the earth, the last soda-water syphon has spluttered abruptly into silence.

My mother goes across the room on that morning of Derby Day 1928. It is fine and sunny, with an air of gentle beginning that promises good things to come. In the Royal College of Music, by the Albert Hall, the usual morning cacophony of voices, violins and pianos has started, and out in the street already the traffic has that look of holiday about it, as though everything, even buses and taxis themselves, is going to Epsom Downs for the day. Down below, just inside Kensington Gardens, the little group of friends has gathered round the mounting block, waiting for the horses. They look up at the house and talk among themselves, as though uncertain whether to send someone over to inquire. Then, as my mother pulls down the blinds (generally used by Lucy to keep the sun off the new mahogany bedsteads), they realize that it is too late and turn away. Everyone in the house is suddenly hushed, except Lucy, who, downstairs in an empty room, audibly laments that she did not think of those thick pants.

FATHER, DEAR FATHER

Chapter I
Barouche

Every afternoon at twenty past five the sound of my father's cab coming up the Worcester Road from Sutton station would reach us in the garden of our house in the Cornwall Road and a perceptible change would come over the household. It was not fear so much as a slight feeling of restraint; a change of atmosphere. Captain Wilson, our tutor, would go through the house raising a cry of 'Barouche! Barouche!' at which my brother and I would cease riding our bicycles round the garden and hastily throw over the next-door fence any flowers which might have been broken or uprooted in the process and, in the last few moments available to us, attempt to do all those jobs about the place that my father had set us on leaving the house in the morning and which had been forgotten or set aside until then.

You may think that a horse cab in the early 1920s is an anachronism, but the half dozen or so that stood outside Sutton station in those days were probably some of the last to be in regular use and they play a large part in the recollections of my childhood because my father was lame. An illness never successfully diagnosed by any of the numerous doctors and quasi-doctors he patronized for the rest of his life struck him down in his thirties and from that time onward he only walked with the help of his two sticks, dragging both feet limply, with a slide and a plop which, if I recall it in my mind, brings back that whole time almost as vividly as one of the popular dance tunes of the period.

Every morning at twenty minutes to nine a cab would come to drive him the mile to Sutton station and the cry of 'Cab's come, Steph!' from my mother would send my brother and me rushing to the dining-room window to see which of the red-faced, bottle-nosed characters, each one a Leach drawing brought to life, had come for him that day.

The cabs themselves, like their drivers, were already museum pieces. In wet weather, with the top up, they were box-like and funereal; but in the sunshine, with the hood down and the passengers half visible – in the case of my father lounging back straw-hatted, pipe in mouth, blandly sunburned – they had an air that was faintly regal, like the royal equipage of some small, seedy Balkan monarchy.

Occasionally on Saturdays, as a special treat, when my

father was not playing bridge at the golf club, the whole family would set off for an afternoon drive over Banstead Downs in the direction of such unknown and exotic-sounding places as Burgh Heath or Chipstead – or the most fabled of all in my father's mind, an area known as 'Little Switzerland' whose whereabouts I still haven't discovered – and we would drag interminably but pleasantly through the Surrey lanes to the somnolent, jog-trot sound of the hoofs, the horsey, leathery smell in one's nostrils while, in my case, being too young to wear long trousers, the horsehair stuffing which burst through the cracked imitation leather of the seats scratched one's unprotected legs and the sun-heated upholstery administered a sharp shock through summer clothing as one sat down.

But to return to our house with its name, Melton, on the front gate. It was small, semi-detached and even by the standards of the early 1900s, when it was probably built, outstandingly ugly. The overall colour was a dark, angry red, but at the same time the builder had managed to incorporate into it as many varying materials as possible. The lower part was red brick and the upper mostly rough caste or 'pebble-dash', though some areas were hung with fancy-shaped pink tiles, while the eaves, which were heavy in the style of the period, were of peeling white paint. The whole house, in fact, had a wan air of debased art nouveau which one still sees in parts of the suburbs. A small, tiled porch led to the front door, the upper part of which was made of variously coloured glass. One section of this – a small circular piece, which should have been crimson, about the size of a tennis ball – was missing. Through this hole, never repaired in our time, my brother and

I would poke anything long enough, such as a bean pole, and push back the catch of the sash window in the hall, making it possible to get into the house at any time without the use of a key; a fact which we were never able to put to its full potential use as our family life as such came to an abrupt end when he was only fourteen and I was about twelve.

The other end of this semi-detached building, the exact complement of Melton, only with, fittingly enough, no hole in the front door, was called Belhaven and was owned by my uncle and aunt. My aunt Mabel was my mother's sister and my uncle, Uncle Ath – believe it or not – was my father's elder brother. Thus it was that, when my aunt Mabel Constanduros later gained fame on the wireless, my mother, to her annoyance, was never able to persuade anybody that she not only had the same married name but was also her actual sister.

Together the two households formed a closely related though, as will be seen, ill-assorted unit; a little world with its own dissentions and rivalries magnified, no doubt, by this close relationship and proximity.

In Melton there was a comparatively raffish, bohemian air, while in Belhaven, under the influence of my uncle, all was tidiness and solvency. Long after my father had rattled home in his cab and was seated in a deckchair in the back garden contemplating his beloved roses, my uncle would still be toiling on foot from the station, having travelled on a later train, carrying in a fish bag some cut-price bargain from the cheaper food shops of the City.

Arriving at the front gate my father would descend slowly from the cab and stand, supported by his two sticks, chatting to the cabman. Once when he was doing this the horse bolted, knocking the cabman, blaspheming, into the gutter, careered up the Cornwall Road with the cab swaying behind it and crashed into somebody's gatepost, thereby bathing our family in a brief notoriety very acceptable to my brother and myself. But as a rule nothing so exciting happened. My father, looking with his button-hole, his bow tie and his generally careless, jaunty air, more like an actor than the architect that he in fact was, would begin his slow progress up the few yards of crazy paving to the front of the porch.

Hearing my father's 'barouche', Captain Wilson would drop the golf club with which he had been practising chip shots over the flowerbeds and hasten indoors. (Here I must pause, once again, to dispel mounting disbelief. A resident tutor in a four-bedroomed semi-detached villa? In the suburbs? In the 1920s? Well, I can only tell you that it was so; and the reasons were quite simple. It was cheaper than sending us both to the local school. The experiment was unique in the district so far as I know. That it was not altogether successful, though it may well have had lasting unexpected results, will appear later.) Putting his hands under the kitchen tap, then running them through his hair to give an appearance of recent exertion, Captain Wilson would meet my father as he let himself in by saying, 'Phew! Hot work cutting that grass on an afternoon like this.'

Dragging himself to the nearest armchair and letting his sticks clatter to the floor my father would wait until he had a good audience then make some dramatic pronouncement.

'Well,' he would say, 'how would you all like to go to South

America?' My mother, busy on some domestic task, would answer, 'Oh yes, dear? I wish you'd do something about these piles of magazines. You said you were going to get them bound, but they've been lying about here on the floor for ages.'

Undeterred my father would continue, 'A chap came into my office today and said "I want to see Constanduros – the expert. I don't want to see any of the others." He's got some big scheme to build a huge hydro-electric dam in Bolivia. If it comes off it'll be something very important for all of us.'

In the days when they were first married my mother used to imagine herself packing up for Madagascar, Cape Cod or wherever it might be that week, but by this time she knew they'd be lucky if they got their usual fortnight at Bognor or Paignton.

Still unabashed my father would drop the subject of foreign travel.

'Oh Norah,' he'd say, 'I've got a little present for you. It's in a parcel on the hall chest.'

'Thank you, Steph dear,' my mother would answer, continuing to pile up the magazines. She knew from experience that this would be smoked cod's roe – which nobody in the house but my father ate.

Chapter II
A Prayer Answered

My father and mother came from totally dissimilar backgrounds. My mother's early life was one of steadily increasing prosperity. The family business, originally a livery stable and riding-school in south London, soon prospered so immensely under the benign but shrewd influence of my grandfather that, branching out into the world of public transport with horse omnibuses, it finally became the largest business of its kind in the London area, looking upon the long since extinct London General Omnibus Company as a mere upstart. From its small family beginnings in the middle of the nineteenth century, through the dangerous transition from horses to motor-cars until its final take-over by the state – on extremely favourable terms to the shareholders – between the wars, the story of its progress seems to typify the whole commercial world of Victorian and Edwardian England. Now it is a vast and prosperous holding company; a company to manage and finance other companies. A far, far cry, one feels, from the dung- and straw-smelling livery stable that my grandfather began with all those years ago in Peckham.

In appearance my grandfather was the exact antithesis of a tycoon. In fact the memory left to those of his grandchildren who knew him is of a small, beaming and utterly benign figure, straight from his beloved and much-quoted Dickens – a kind of minor Pickwick or Cheeryble brother. But great enterprises cannot be built on amiability alone. In his early, struggling days the commercial iron must have been somewhere in my grandfather's soul. Proof of it lies in the fact that there grew up within his large and loving family a secret, subversive element, a kind of anti-commercial underground movement, entirely feminine in origin and feeling, and headed, one suspects, at least covertly, by my grandmother. As the houses they inhabited in South London became successively larger and the servants more numerous this secret underground feeling grew. It was not the luxury that my grandmother and her daughters rebelled against in spirit; it was the whole masculine commercial world with its interminable discussions of 'capital', 'turnover' and 'hidden assets', the world of the 'sound chap' and the company prospectus in its long brown envelope on the breakfast table.

This was the world from which my mother and her sisters dissented. It was not a revolt of the unhappy or the repressed but merely an expression of the human spirit, at first in the nursery and later at those feminine conclaves that take place at night in the privacy of bathrooms and bedrooms. 'Preserve me', they muttered to each other alone, upstairs, 'from marrying a businessman.' In the case of my mother at least this prayer was answered with embarrassing exactitude.

My father first appeared on the scene when he was in his late twenties and my mother was a girl of about fifteen. Everything must have been in his favour; he was charming, slightly foreign in origin, handsome in a romantic way and, above all, poor. His own father had been a political *émigré* from Greece who had married an Englishwoman and settled down to a precarious existence in a poor part of south London. Their children were called Helena, Athene, Constantine, Leonidas, Athanasius (as in the Creed, my Uncle Ath from next door) and the youngest (my father), Stephanos.

My Greek grandfather, who died long before I was born, never learned to speak English properly. How he managed to provide for this large family I have no idea. The story that my father told us was that most of his family were killed in a political rising of some sort and that my grandfather escaped to Turkey, coming later to London where he was said to have had some sort of job in the Turkish Embassy. Beyond feeling a slight, snobbish pride at having a foreign name and being therefore to some extent different from the others at school I had no interest whatever in my Greek antecedents and never thought to ask even the most elementary questions about them. Now there is no one left who knows their story.

While the elder members of my father's family seem to have had a normal education, one suspects that the *émigré* business had ceased to thrive by the time it came to my father's turn. Fortunately he had a number of gifts which more than made up for this; the chief among them being a remarkable singing voice. As a boy he had considerable success as a soloist and, when his voice broke, he sang professionally for some time.

This, coupled with his foreign appearance, made it easy for him to dispense with a formal education and for a while he seems to have knocked around in a dubious world that included such varied characters as a West End art dealer, an ex-jockey and a professional strong man, whose exploit in uprooting a slot-machine from the pavement and carrying it home after an evening party won our unstinted admiration as boys and was only seen in its full implications in after years.

About this time one of his friends, an older man and a qualified architect, offered him a job in his office. So my father, among whose other natural talents was an ability to draw, became an architect. How he qualified – or indeed if he did – I do not know. But an architect he was and a number of quite respectable buildings by the standards of the period remained in London, at least until quite recently, to prove it.

But on the evening when he first appeared at the supper table in my mother's family house, after playing in a local cricket match, he had no apparent future prospects of any kind. Tall, dark, athletic and totally at ease on all occasions in spite of the supposedly insurmountable handicap of having no money, to the fifteen-year-old girl who sat at the end of the table among her sisters he must have represented all that was romantic and forbidden. After supper, in the drawing-room, he sang. Relaxed, hand carelessly in pocket, imperturbable – once, while in full song, standing under a lighted gas jet, his hair caught fire but he continued singing undisturbed – he charmed them all. Not least my grandfather who, always susceptible to the emotional stimulus of music, jumped up from his seat, clapped his hands and cried out 'Bravo! Bravo!' – a spontaneous reaction which, if he remembered it, he must have regretted to the end of his life.

Small wonder that my mother, with the secret of her anti-commercial rebellion burning within her, was impressed. If my grandfather, notorious discourager of marriageable young men, should approve then surely she could feel herself free to do the same? That night the bedroom that she shared with her sister Mabel shone with my father's name, painted in blue on the gas globe; the highest honour possible and awarded only to a very few.

From this point the friendship between my mother and father was developed largely in secret – always an unfailing stimulus to romance. He would wait for her after her confirmation classes, which were about the only occasions when she was allowed out alone, and together they would loiter back through the twilit streets of south London and part, judiciously, at the end of the road.

Photographs of the period show the sisters as stodgy, pale girls, too richly fed, too heavily clothed, reclining on the ornamental seats of a south London garden. One catches, even at this distance of time, a faint whiff of the frustrations, mental and physical, of the moment. Looking at them one feels, perhaps with too much hindsight, that they were frozen in a perpetual Sunday afternoon of repletion and ennui. If they were it was certainly to some extent unconscious. They were happy; they loved their enclosed family life, with its private world of jokes and shared romances, they loved their parents, if one can call love that mixture of obsession and enmity which all growing children feel for those who have put on them a permanent sense of obligation by causing their existence. Yet somewhere behind those seemingly expressionless faces, whose placid, digestive stare is all that remains to communicate with the present-day viewer, there lurked the basic feminine conviction that all this business of wealth and the acquisition of it, of aggression, competition and display, is childish and that the real business of living is something other. Unconsciously, one suspects, they longed for the healthy, life-giving stimulus of insecurity. In my mother's case at least it was not long coming.

Soon after my father's first appearance at the house they somehow managed to become engaged. The moment approached when my mother, obeying the dictates of the time, was obliged to show her parents the ring. My grandfather was in his study smoking an after-dinner cigar and reading *The Times*. The original pleasure he had felt when my father first sang had long since evaporated, all too soon to be replaced by the normal feeling of alarm occasioned in the hearts of all fathers of daughters at the sight of a young man, exaggerated to the near-panic of the wealthy at the approach of the impecunious. Besides, in his own way, my grandfather had a special affection for his daughters and would probably have hated them leaving home even if they had married wealthy men; though this was never actually put to the test.

On this occasion my mother pushed open the door of my grandfather's room with some reluctance. Normally the study was forbidden ground. Once inside my grandfather was incommunicado, safe from the noise and foolishness of his children, only to be visited on special occasions and by appointment. This, of course, was a very special occasion and my grandfather had evidently been forewarned. Plucking up her courage my mother came in and said, 'I've got something to show you, Papa.'

'Thank you, my dear,' he answered, puffing at his cigar, 'I

don't want to see it.' And he went back to the financial page of *The Times*. The matter was never again referred to – at any rate more than is strictly necessary when making the arrangements for a large and formal wedding.

My father, by then a practising architect, designed and built a new house for his bride in the then flourishing district of Sutton. This was not the semi-detached monstrosity of the Cornwall Road but a much more pretentious building of many gables and wide, shallow-pitched roofs with a fair-sized garden which included, of course, a tennis court. He not only designed the house but much of the furniture and fittings as well, which were specially made – even the mirrors and fire-irons. Here, during the first year of their married life, they gave the dinner and tennis parties expected of a well-to-do young couple. My mother, who had survived a full and happy childhood without acquiring the smallest domestic knowledge of any kind, was obliged to ring up my grandmother as each new difficulty of married life presented itself, even to the extent of asking the difference between mutton and beef, while my father, not yet stricken down with his mysterious illness, spent what leisure time he could spare from his garden at the golf club. If my mother had any secret hopes that she was escaping from middle-class respectability into *la vie de bohème* she must have been very disappointed. My father clearly had every intention of making her married life a replica in miniature of what it had been before. He succeeded in every respect but one. When they had been married a little more than a year he confessed to my mother that he'd spent his last ha'penny and had no idea where the next was coming from.

Chapter III
My Father Cries 'Wolf' – or Does He?

To the ordinary worldly observer, therefore, it must have seemed quite obvious that my father married his wife for her money; that he was in fact an adventurer. After all he was twelve years older, already a man about town in a minor way, used to the company of an odd collection of acquaintances in the theatrical and sporting worlds, while she was mentally if not actually almost a child. By most standards he had done very well for himself.

Yet in my opinion this would be unjust to him. With all his faults he was never mercenary or scheming; indeed we might well have done better as a family if he had been. My mother, puzzling over the question many years later, decided that he married her simply because she was fair. All his own family, with their Mediterranean antecedents, were very dark and, so she maintained, the sight of fair hair and blue eyes was particularly pleasing to him. It seems a good enough reason; though fair hair is not uncommon in England and it appears strange that he hadn't noticed any before. (In the same speculative vein she later decided that her sister Mabel had married Uncle Ath to make sure of a supper partner at dances. Perhaps she had a tendency to over-simplification.)

It seems reasonable to suppose and quite in character that, having married a girl from a prosperous family, he simply lacked courage to admit straight out that they couldn't afford several maids and a gardener. So many things start with seemingly small evasions that grow and multiply in secret like a mental cancer. The bills that my father soon began opening below the level of the breakfast table mounted rapidly. The effect was cumulative. Unable to meet his obligations financially his only reply was ill health. Soon after they were married my father woke up suddenly in the middle of the night and cried out dramatically, 'Norah! Norah! I'm choking! I'm dying!'

My mother was very alarmed. In the world she came from if people said they were dying they died. She stumbled downstairs and rang the family doctor, who took a more objective view.

The next time he woke up choking she didn't send for the doctor until the morning, and by the time they had been married a few years she merely answered in a conversational tone, 'Go on then, die,' and went off to sleep again.

So when, still in the fairly early days of their marriage, he went to bed for a week and announced that he'd lost the use of his legs, nobody took it too tragically. Yet from that time – before I can remember – he never again walked without the help of two sticks. Golf, tennis and gardening were, of course, out of the question. So were such simple matters as walking to and from the station. From that day onward the routine of the morning and evening cab was established. His working day at the office became even shorter which, needless to say, instead of helping to evade the financial issue merely made it worse. Naturally everything was tried to cure him. He began a round of doctors and nursing homes, both genuinely medical and quack, finishing up with a long course of Christian Science, but he continued to walk slowly on his two sticks, dragging his limp feet, toes hanging downward, with the familiar 'slip' and 'plop' which became the leitmotif of our family life.

The charitable answer now appears to be that my father had a mild attack of polio; though why none of the innumerable doctors he went to ever even suggested it I don't know. Looking back now one feels inclined to give him the benefit of the doubt; yet it was the very existence of this doubt, hanging over the household, which gave the particular flavour to the whole of our family life as I remember it. As a child one accepts as normal whatever circumstances one finds oneself born into. It seemed quite unremarkable to me that my father should walk with two sticks, that nobody should be able to decide what was wrong with him – indeed whether anything at all was wrong with him – that bills should not be paid and that everything in our house should be shabbier and more broken than in the houses of the friends we played with – just as the record of 'The Sword and Lance March' played on our old gramophone with its blue tin horn sounded 'right', while the same record on the truer gramophones of our friends sounded 'wrong'.

To add to the enigma my father's basic health remained exceptionally good. Bronzed, handsome, unlined, he would heave his twelve or thirteen stone into the bath-chair we always had to hire for him on our summer holidays and lie back, rotund, at peace with the world, his straw hat at an angle, his pipe in his mouth and his spotted bow tie slightly askew while my mother pushed him laboriously to the beach and back and my brother and myself trotted along beside, quite unmoved by pity or criticism of any kind, merely waiting for the moment when my father had heaved himself out of the chair and we could give each other rides up and down the promenade at the greatest possible speed.

This, then, was roughly the situation when I became old enough to observe and remember this for myself. Everybody's early life is like a television play switched on casually halfway through. One has to pick up the threads of the plot, decide for oneself from various clues who are the villains and who the heroes. All that has gone before is guesswork, or at the best hearsay, coloured by the particular bias of the teller. I make no claim, therefore, that the account that I have given so far is fair. Of course it isn't. Nor, no doubt, are my recollections of later events fair; yet the prejudice itself is part of the story.

Chapter IV
An Armstrong Siddeley at the Gate

It was soon obvious even to my father that in Mount Mascal, the house he designed and built for their family life, he had bitten off more than he could chew. By this time our fortunes were already steeply on the decline. Of course such things were never discussed in front of my brother and myself, so my assessment of the situation is mostly guesswork, based on later knowledge of the parties concerned.

My grandfather, by the sound of things, refused to help any further and decided that his vocally pleasing but otherwise unsatisfactory son-in-law was to be left to find his own financial level; which, when one looks back, proved to be pretty low. My earliest recollections are of a series of gloomy furnished houses – St Cyre's, Peveril and later our final house, Melton – each within an area of about a quarter of a mile from the other, on the borders of Sutton and Cheam and each, in my recollection, a little shabbier than the last. But behind all this, singling us out, we secretly felt, from our more obviously respectable neighbours, lay the enormous, ever-present fact of my grandfather's wealth.

Let us try to be perfectly honest. Children are in many ways primitive creatures. If I was not particularly conscious of my own shabbiness – our shabbiness was somehow better than other people's smartness simply because it was ours –

then admittedly the sight of my grandfather's chauffeur-driven Armstrong Siddeley standing outside our front gate certainly gave us a kind of distinction. Privately owned motor cars were still a rarity in the Cornwall Road. During our stay there we never reached the point of owning one. It was therefore to some extent the desire for peculiarity, something to distinguish one from all the other families, mostly unknown to us, who were our neighbours, and not merely as a symbol of wealth that my grandfather's car was such a reassuring sight.

Another valuable distinguishing mark was, of course, my father's lameness. Nobody else's father in the Cornwall Road walked with two sticks and went to the station in a cab. Nobody else, so far as we knew, had a name that could never be understood over the telephone or correctly spelt even when apparently understood. There was the splendid moment, already mentioned, of my father's bolting cab, and the occasion later when he was arrested as a German spy for sketching an upturned boat during our summer holiday at Selsey. The policeman, on hearing his name, became so suspicious that for one glorious day we had a uniformed officer placed opposite the villa in which we had 'rooms'. Distinction could hardly have gone further.

But to return to my grandfather's Armstrong Siddeley. Once a year, at Christmas, it arrived to transport us the few miles that separated the Cornwall Road from his large and I now realize gloomy house on Sydenham Hill, with its vast, park-like garden down whose empty asphalt paths, winding through dank grottoes, I still sometimes find myself running in dreams. The inside of the house, too, comes back to me sometimes and always frighteningly, with long, unlit passages down which one must go to bed, far beyond the call of grown-ups, safely downstairs chattering away in the brightly lit drawing-room, while a full-length mirror reflects one's frightened, ghostly face and the cavernous darkness of the passage behind.

Each Christmas we were bidden from our current villa to the fleshpots of Sydenham Hill, where for a few days we enjoyed the good life, waited on by family servants. On wet afternoons, when the sky was low and the great empty garden closed to us, our chief joy was the billiard room, with the solemn table discreetly draped in our presence, its batteries of shaded lights glaringly dramatically down as on the scene of some religious rite – a specifically masculine rite, one felt. Built into the corners of the room were large horse-hair settees, raised on small platforms, from which, presumably, spectators – even women – might observe these rites. Round the walls were hunting and coaching prints by Cecil Aldin, an upright rack with spring clips to hold billiard cues and a particularly intriguing 'smoking table' of unvarnished Swiss wood, with a cigarette or cigar box made to look like a log cabin. There was also an HMV gramophone with a wooden horn and a collection of 12-inch, single-sided records (the ubiquitous Fritz Kreisler playing 'Humoresque' and 'Tambourin Chinois', or Harry Lauder singing 'Stop Your Tickling Jock').

But best of all in our eyes was the pianola, at which one pumped away with one's feet while the piano stool slid gradually backward on the polished parquet and the keys mysteriously bobbed up and down on their own as though played by invisible fingers.

When at last the Armstrong Siddeley returned us to the Cornwall Road it was to a house that seemed suddenly to have shrunk and become pitifully threadbare. But this hallucination – or lack of it – would soon wear off and after a day or two our own house and garden were once again the true standards of measurement; anything larger was vulgar and anything smaller mean and contemptible.

Chapter V
Rival Households

All my recollections of this period are coloured by the first war. My father standing at the window in the night, watching the searchlights criss-crossing over London, while the Gothas droned unevenly in the distance and a piece of shrapnel rattled down the roof of the house opposite. My father returning triumphant in his cab with a tiny piece of meat, won by his own irresistible charm we were sure, in the face of all opposition. My father gleefully reading the lists of all those prosecuted for 'food hoarding', with special relish when he came upon somebody personally known to us.

About the middle of the war, no doubt for financial reasons, the households of the two brothers united under a single roof. We abandoned our descent from furnished house to furnished house and moved into Belhaven, the counterpart of the hideous Melton next door, which was later to be the scene of our final phase.

I was too young, fortunately, to realize all the tensions this almost incestuous overcrowding must have caused, because, though my mother and her sister Mabel were the best of friends all their lives, my father and his brother Ath had nothing whatever in common.

Uncle Ath was small, hard-working and above all solvent, none of which adjectives applied to my father. I can see him best in my mind's eye on winter Saturdays, when he went beagling, dressed in a belted Norfolk jacket and knickerbockers. In the evening he would come home and, over a boiled egg with his tea, recount at great length how 'He (the hare) turned left-handed, leaving Merstham Church as it were here, by this sugar basin, and struck away across the plough in the direction of Godstone . . .' Or whatever it might be.

I'm afraid nobody listened, for, to be quite honest, Uncle Ath was something of a bore and, looking back, it was this I suspect that underlay my father's scarcely concealed contempt. Children are always extremely quick to pick up the undertone of feeling between the grown-ups who surround them, though the causes are naturally as a rule beyond them. Uncle Ath, with his small man's habit of 'making an entrance' as he came into a room, throwing back his head to survey the company underneath his gold-rimmed spectacles, was, in our more raffish family, looked upon as something of a figure of fun – a kind of latter-day Mr Pooter.

Yet in other ways I think we held him in a degree of secret affection, because he supplied for us many things that our own father could not. He would bowl to us in the back garden by the hour, high donkey-drops with a tennis ball, using an elegantly old-fashioned, round-arm action. Or again, when we were playing on our own and the ball, as it inevitably did, went on the flowerbeds, my father, waking from an apparent reverie in his deckchair the moment one's toe had touched the forbidden earth, would suddenly roar: 'Here – boy! Come off that bed at once!' – even when not under stress he could never remember our Christian names – while if the same thing happened in the Belhaven garden Uncle Ath would merely pause, spade in hand, and say, with a pained expression, 'I'd rather you didn't do that old chap, if you don't mind,' shake his head sadly and go on digging.

My aunt Mabel – 'Pix' to all her family, we never called her 'aunt' – was also small and if, in a sense, she was also something of a family joke it was a role she deliberately courted and played up as hard as she could. Already she had achieved local celebrity at charity concerts, performing her own cockney monologues. People said she should 'go on the stage', but it was still some years before the wireless suddenly drew her out of her suburban obscurity and transformed her whole life.

Vivacious and sociable, her desire to please and astonish would often dismay her more literal-minded sister. If the vicar called she would be amazed to hear Pix deeply engaged in a discussion of the efficacy of prayer – though she never went with her husband to church – and the poor parson would go away convinced that he had made a convert. If the caller was a woman she would be suitably domestic.

'I always give my fruit cakes a good hour and a half in a slow oven,' she would say, regardless of the fact that she never went near the kitchen. 'Pix's cakes' became another family joke.

Again, walking through the garden with an enthusiast, my mother once heard her say: 'And that's a Granny Smith. It doesn't really do very well here. But then of course it's always a shy fruiter.'

Until that moment none of her family realized that she knew the difference between an apple and an oak tree. And 'shy fruiter'. Where in the world had she picked that up? The maddening part about it was that, though she took such wild risks, she hardly ever came a cropper. She nearly always got it right. 'Pix!' my mother would exclaim with horror, after some particularly outrageous statement, 'You know it didn't happen like that.'

'Oh well,' she'd reply, brushing aside such a feeble objection, 'you've got to make a good story or it's better not to say anything at all.'

The most disarming thing about her was that she loved these family legends about herself, collecting, preserving and probably embellishing them as much as anyone.

Looking back now she and Uncle Ath seem so oddly ill-assorted that one can hardly think of them as a pair. Uncle Ath, a stickler for the literal truth and enemy of all change, could never accept Summer Time, first introduced during the 1914–18 war. Though he did finally consent to alter the dining-room clock he got his own back on those in authority by writing 'Government Time, not Real Time' on a postcard which he propped against one of the Cornish marble vases on the mantelshelf, where it remained for some years.

He also stuck stamp paper over the cracks that appeared in bathroom and lavatory walls, writing the date neatly in his exemplary handwriting, presumably to see whether the cracks widened; though my brother and I, no doubt encouraged by our father, professed to believe that it was to hold the house together.

A household so overcrowded with divergent yet inter-related people could hardly hope to survive for long. Sunday lunch, as I remember, was particularly trying. (But then who hasn't early recollections of dreadful Sunday lunchtimes?) Uncle Ath, tilting back his head to see below his glasses, would begin a long story while carefully carving the minute wartime joint, describing at extreme length how, while processing down the aisle with the rest of the choir, he happened to notice that one of the tiles on the floor was slightly out of position and how he very nearly – but not quite – tripped over it; breaking off occasionally to say to my brother or myself, 'I won't give you too much, old fellow, because I know you aren't hungry.' Or, if the story continued into the pudding course, seeing my brother's eye straying round the table, he would suddenly pause and say, 'Sickly sweet, old chap. You won't want any sugar.'

Not surprisingly this experiment in communal family living was fairly brief. In the winter of 1917, at the height – or depth – of the war our family suddenly altered course and left the safe, suburban world of the Cornwall Road and plunged into the then almost uncharted wilds on the edge of Salisbury Plain – to a charmingly dilapidated farmhouse in the village of Collingbourne Ducis. The motive for this now seems obscure; but whatever the reasons I only know that for one member of the small band that set out from the Cornwall Road the love affair with Wiltshire has lasted a lifetime.

Chapter VI
Lizzie

Here, I'm afraid, there must be a pause and a slight digression. On trying to recall that party which set out for Collingbourne I realize that, though my father was only able to visit us at weekends because his work kept him in London, it consisted not only of us two boys and my mother, but also of Lizzie.

It is typical, too, that Lizzie should only have emerged from the shades so late and so unobtrusively, for Lizzie was a servant. One can hardly bring oneself to write the ugly word now, but it must in honesty be done. Lizzie was a servant. There! She was, in fact, what was known as a 'cook-general', which merely meant that our household was so small and humble that, besides the cooking, she had to do as many other jobs about the house as she could manage.

I can see her now, in the fusty cap and apron of her office, her face pale and permanently expressionless, hurrying about the kitchen with her head slightly on one side, bent on preparing or clearing up the meals which we accepted as a matter of course. She never, to my knowledge, complained; in fact she seldom, to my recollection, spoke. As a family we thought highly of her cooking – Lizzie's steak-and-kidney pudding later became part of the Melton ethos – but of her as a person we never thought at all.

It seems quite extraordinary now, and a matter for some

embarrassment and shame, that in that small, semi-detached villa another human being could exist day after day, year after year, about whom one had not the faintest curiosity. As children, so far as we thought of her at all, we quite liked her; while she, so far as she thought about us, probably felt the same. She must have had feelings of some sort. She must have been some particular kind of person and of a particular age; yet in my recollection of her this is not so.

Looking back now one sees the conditions under which we co-existed, the taboos and boundary lines, as quite fascinating. In the small, dark kitchen with its coal cooking range and gas-fired Potterton boiler for heating the water, Lizzie was paramount. ('Just ask Lizzie to light the Potterton dear, if you want a bath,' or 'Don't bother Lizzie just now, dear, she's getting the dinner.') Yet in other parts of the house she became, as I say, more or less anonymous. It was really a kind of unspoken, unrealized form of apartheid, or separate development. But in case that emotive word should push you into a preconceived response, please believe that this was never imposed on an unwilling or resentful recipient. It was accepted as unquestioningly by one side as the other.

Lizzie's bedroom was, appropriately enough, separated from ours by a few steps and was on a slightly lower level. It was also down at the end of a small unlighted passage and next to the lavatory – 'our' lavatory, not hers. 'Her' lavatory was in the yard, just outside the back door. I can never remember any one of the family using it – indeed to do so would have been to violate every unspoken code of conduct and I don't think the idea even entered our heads – not because to do so would have been beneath our dignity but simply because it was 'hers'.

The same applied to her bedroom. I think I only saw inside it about twice in all the years we lived there. And this was not just a matter of propriety, because we were boys and she was – presumably – of a somewhat different sex; it was because it was 'her' room, her territory, where, one now likes to feel, she could have her own shamefully proscribed and limited existence, undisturbed.

Poor Lizzie – the only thing I can remember about her background and her early life was that she came from Northampton, that her father worked in a boot factory and that when times were bad all they had to eat was bread and dripping. ('What is she grumbling about?' I can remember thinking. 'We only have bread and dripping as a special treat.')

I can also remember that, later, when we were all at Collingbourne, there was one tiny thatched cottage, about two-up-and-two-down, standing back from the village street, which she happened to say she would like to live in. It is the only statement, the only manifestation of a personal desire, that I can actually recall her making. Today it still stands, and I still think of it as 'Lizzie's cottage'.

Later, when we were in our final phase at Melton, she was courted, to her own surprise as much as everyone else's, by a large, red-faced and speechless builder's labourer. After a long, and one can only suppose silent, wooing they were married. It was the end of an epoch at Melton. It was more than that for Lizzie. After a few grim years in the back streets of the hinterland between Sutton and Croydon, and about as far in spirit from her Wiltshire cottage as it would be possible to conceive, she died giving birth to his second child.

It seems shocking now to think of anyone being condemned to live a life so dim; of somebody whose demands and expectations were so humble and negligible, yet who so hopelessly failed to realize them. Looking back over the last fifty years one feels that the Lizzies of this world and the response, or lack of it, that they evoked were far more significant than is often realized. The idea that one human being should be the 'servant' of another, in the old, biblical sense, is now rightly repugnant to most people. Service in a big house, where those who live below stairs and are part of a community, with its own laws and structure, is another matter altogether. The single, living-in servant in the small house, privileged slave, semi-friend yet social outcast, is happily a thing of the past, yet the feeling of guilt that they left behind in the middle class of this country is something that I suspect has had a profound effect on the social history of the time, and is still doing so.

Chapter VII
Winter Journey

It was mid-winter and still wartime when we made our exodus from the safe familiarity of Sutton to the unknown world of rural Wiltshire. The details of the trip have gone from me; but any train journey involving, as this did, several changes and a final arrival, past one's normal bedtime, at a small and ill-lit country station was an adventure in itself.

It was nearly dark when at last we arrived, dazed and exhausted, in the lane outside the Hermitage, the house where we were to spend the winter; and to add to the romance of the occasion it had been snowing. The house – L-shaped and old – lay some distance back from the road and one approached it through an iron gate, up a flight of uneven brick steps and then by way of a garden path flanked on both sides by a dwarf box hedge. Everywhere one looked the garden seemed an exciting tangle of untrimmed ivy and ancient, twisted yew trees; a teeming, overgrown, mysterious place, full of friendliness and promise and, as we pushed open the squeaking iron gate and climbed the brick steps, it seemed to have that magical quality of total stillness that one only finds immediately after snow has fallen.

To us, previously, the word 'garden' had meant a flat, rectangular piece of ground, bordered by a fence on the other side of which lay an exactly similar-sized rectangle belonging to some unknown, possibly hostile, race of beings who refused to throw one's ball back. Garden paths, mostly made of crazy paving and cut in straight lines – or 'artistically' curved for no visible reason – would be spanned at regular intervals by rustic-work arches covered in Dorothy Perkins roses, leading from and to nowhere in particular. Lawns, when not sacred to tennis, were cut up by symmetrical circular or diamond-shaped beds bordered by pansies or pinks.

The only other garden we knew was the one on Sydenham Hill, with its winding asphalt paths and its flitting, screeching jays, so large as to be slightly sinister, like an uninhabited park.

In spite of its air of chaos and neglect there was nothing faintly sinister about the Hermitage garden. Its secret places were many and rewarding. Everywhere one went one found the lost balls or decomposing rag-dolls of previous generations, for it was a garden that presented an open welcome to all children and seemed to come alive only at the sound of their voices.

But all this was as yet unknown to us as we trudged, like a band of explorers, through the virgin snow of the garden path. Before us the house lay dark and ivy-covered, its windows latticed and its roof irregular. Almost fearfully, my mother led the way through the back door and into the stone-flagged kitchen. Looking back I can imagine that morale must have been extremely low at that moment – though worse was to come.

My recollection of that house is that it was enormous. No doubt in comparison with Melton and Belhaven it was; yet I suspect that it was muddly rather than large. Everything seemed to be on different levels. Two steps would lead to a short, brick-floored passage; two more into a damp-smelling room containing nothing but some rotting shelves and a large cistern. Everywhere there seemed to be doors, some leading normally from one room to another; some, ill-fitting and hard to open, merely to dark, evil-smelling cupboards, while under several layers of peeling wallpaper lay the unmistakable traces of yet others, long since sealed up. It was a house of doors, both functional and non-functional, and therefore a house of draughts. The kitchen floor was worn by generations of farm boots into depressions, especially in the doorways, through which the wind rushed unchecked; yet it was so damp that fungus and mildew grew overnight, like a tropical plant. Jets of icy air shot from holes in the floorboards, mats lifted as though by levitation as the steady ground-current surged from room to room.

That winter coal was almost unobtainable and we had to make do with hissing logs. The oil lamps afterwards added a welcome warmth – in a small room with a low ceiling they make a remarkable difference as well as giving the gentlest and pleasantest of all forms of light – yet on that first evening my mother had no notion how to use them, so we had to make do with candles. Shielding their candles as best they could from the blasts which greeted them round every corner my mother and Lizzie explored, while we sat shivering and half asleep in the kitchen. Down the brick-paved passage they found the empty, damp-smelling room that contained the cistern. This, they discovered, supplied a primitive and forbidding-looking sink with a single brass tap, also – an unexpected bonus – an ancient but recognizable lavatory next door.

They turned the brass tap over the sink. Nothing happened. They pulled the lavatory chain. Nothing happened. Climbing on to a chair, candle aloft, my mother peered into the cistern. It was empty. The reason for this at last became apparent. There was a pipe at the bottom for letting water out; there was no pipe at the top for letting water in.

Truth began to dawn. It would have to be filled by hand. Taking their guttering candles they finally found, in an outhouse, a well with a rope and bucket. Even by daylight there is something ominous about a well. At night, in the strange surroundings of a dank, slippery well house, it must have seemed to my town-bred mother and Lizzie forbidding in the extreme. Goaded by necessity they lowered the bucket; not rapidly, with a hand on the rope to check its speed, as one afterwards saw the experts do, but laboriously, turn by turn. At last, echoing from the darkness below they heard a splash as the bucket hit the water. Eagerly they began to wind. One turn told them the truth – the bucket had come off the hook.

So began our Wiltshire winter – the coldest of my recollection. From a practical point of view the Hermitage had almost every disadvantage it is possible for a house to have – and of course my brother and I loved it at first sight.

Chapter VIII
Noob

That winter surely was the coldest in living memory – or so it seemed at the Hermitage – yet I remember it as the happiest period of our family life. In a way the intense cold seemed to be part of the happiness. At night, going to bed, tooth water slopped on to the marble top of the washstand in one's bedroom froze as it fell and the tooth glass would glide crazily out of control; but downstairs, in the dimly lit rooms, by a hissing log fire, there was a primitive sense of cosiness and security.

Every day my brother and I, exploring the garden, would make some new discovery – an ivy-covered door in the garden wall, arched and ecclesiastical with dark stained glass, long

since unopenable; an overgrown flight of steps leading into
the next-door farmyard; and, of course, an unlimited amount
of buried treasure. In those days refuse collections, as well as
drainage, in a country district were an unheard-of luxury and
each house existed on a rich deposit of its own waste products
animal, vegetable and mineral. Entwined among the elder
bushes that formed part of the boundary with the adjoining
farmyard one found the ends of iron bedsteads, while one
only had to stick a fork into the ground to turn up the aspirin
bottles, decaying rags and rusty wheels of a previous civilization which we lumped together under the general name of
'Bicycle manure'. It was slightly before the era of the tin can
but even so, much of what one used was indestructible, and
we soon found ourselves adding our own contribution. For
the benefit of future generations, we left, in one forgotten corner, a small notice saying, 'Jug Buried Here'.

The world of 1917, even for children, was totally dominated
by the war. My mother had bought for us khaki 'Tommy's
suits, complete with puttees that had to be wound and those
formless caps that immediately date all photographs of the
period. We lived in them, and my recollection of that time
was of breaking off from our explorations to run down and
lean over the wall as the approaching sound of tramping feet
and singing told us that another route march from Tidworth
or Perham Down was going by in the lane below. Resting our
elbows on the wall we'd watch in secret until the last, faint
sound of 'Good-bye-ee' or 'There's a Long, Long Trail a
Winding' had dwindled into nothing and the village resumed
its normal intermittent sounds, of cartwheels, the thick, inar-

ticulate voice of a carter and the occasional crowing of a cock.

We'd return to our interrupted game, whatever it was, yet for some time there would be a sense of loss and anti-climax, like a theatre when the performance is over and the audience has gone home.

I can remember no sense of tragedy or the awfulness of the time. Those cheerfully marching troops had no significance for us other than a temporary lifting of the spirit and quickening of the pulse. For the adults it must have been a particularly dark time; yet I remember it as one of blissful happiness – in fact the last unadulterated happiness of my childhood.

We were by now at an age when, in present times, a child would be obliged by law to go to school. No such law seems to have existed then, or if it did my parents chose to ignore it. Instead they engaged for us a governess, Miss Newby, or 'Noob', as she soon became.

She was a tall, thin woman with a pointed nose and hair drawn back in a bun. She wore shapeless home-knitted cardigans, extremely long skirts and ropes of beads the same colour as her eyes, which were blue. Fairness compels me to say that she was the vulgar, seaside postcard version of that most maligned character, the English spinster of modest means – in fact she was a cliché come to life. Yet like most clichés, this one disclosed only part of the truth. In her gentle, maidenly way Noob had a good sense of humour and indeed was much more human than her appearance might have led one to suspect.

Lessons, in the morning only, were nominal. She did her best to make us speak French as though it was a foreign language and not a perverted form of English; but our native self-consciousness defeated her. We could never bring our mouths to form those embarrassingly affected sounds.

The afternoons were devoted to enormous walks. 'Going for a walk' is now a special and peculiar activity; then it was the only way of getting out of the village. We hadn't quite reached the stage when we owned bicycles. (That was to come soon enough.) There were two main walks, in opposite directions and with different characteristics, yet they had one thing in common – both had unobtainable objectives. If you went east out of the village, up a chalky lane that finally dwindled into turf at the beginning of the downs – up 'Cadley' as it was called locally – you then plunged into the dark and seemingly unending Collingbourne Woods, probably at one time a part of nearby Savernake Forest. The objective on this walk was a village called Chute.

We never got there. I suppose it exists. At any rate there it still is on the map. No doubt there are people walking about it as I write this who have actually been there – and come safely back. I have not. Motor transport has made almost everything possible. I suppose at any moment in my later, adult life I could have said 'Today I will drive to Chute.' I have not; and will not. Let it remain one of the unexplored mysteries of childhood – Chute, the Wiltshire Shangri La.

But if we never achieved the declared goal, there was a lesser one that was almost as attractive. In a small clearing in the middle of the wood there was a dew pond, and this dew pond was full of newts. These were collected in jam-jars and brought home to live in a galvanized bath in the Hermitage garden where, on many mornings in that hard winter, one had to remove half an inch of solid ice before feeding them.

Again it never seems to have occurred to anyone that the newts must have found their new life extremely restricted. We were not intentionally cruel; we loved our newts and followed their fortunes with a paternal interest; yet an interest not sufficiently enlightened to take them back and empty the jam-jars into the pond again, as in retrospect one wishes one had.

If the way through the woods was dark and enclosed – suitable for a mood of introspection – our other walk was exactly the opposite. It went in a westerly direction, towards the early setting sun, up Chick's Lane towards the village of Everley, hidden in an oasis of trees in the rolling, hedgeless country that is the beginning of Salisbury Plain.

Up across downland cart-tracks we'd go, past a ruin known as Old Ann's Barn, with lines of peewits strung out over the ploughed fields, while away in the distance, towards the huge, wintry sun just beyond the next ridge as it seemed, aeroplanes were landing and taking off – SE5s, Sopwith Camels with their slightly upswept lower wings, old Avros, easy to spot with their ski-like landing skid in the undercarriage. (We were aircraft fanatics and knew them all. In fact to this day the sound of a 'period' engine – say the old 'Gnome-Le-Rhône' rotary used in the fighters of the time, is almost as evocative as a recording of Violet Lorraine in *The Bing Boys*. I may add that my knowledge of aircraft stops abruptly at about the year 1920.)

'Just to the top of that next hill,' we would say, tugging at Noob's arm. 'Oh let's! Come on, it's not far.'

And off we would go, to find, at the top of the next rise, the same rolling plain, the same aircraft landing and taking off just out of sight over a still inaccessible horizon.

In the end even we would have to admit defeat and we would trail home through the dusk in the keen, frosty air – our grins frozen – to a high tea in the Hermitage kitchen and afterwards, perhaps, on very special occasions, a bath.

Nowadays having a bath seems nothing to get excited about. One has them all the time. Yet I honestly believe that no millionaire, no oil sheikh even, could possibly know the sheer luxury of a hip-bath in one's bedroom, before a crackling wood fire, with cans of hot water wrapped in towels to keep them warm and another towel to step out on as one dried oneself in the firelight.

Luxury, yes, if it was not you who had to heat those cans on the kitchen range, carry them upstairs and, when the bath was over, reverse the process by bailing and tipping the water out and carrying it all down again.

Yet luxurious as it was there was another side to it. Crouching there alone in the hip-bath could be an eerie business for a child of six or seven, with the firelight dancing on the ceiling and the dark corners of the room charged with menace, while, to add to it, if it was a Thursday, the ringers would be practising in the nearby church and the sound of the bells would come intermittently, now far away, then suddenly, borne on the wind, ominously near in a clashing jangle of noise which made the spine tingle and the heart beat faster.

During Noob's term of office one thing soon became apparent; she adored my brother. Even in one's nursery days

triangles tend to arise. In a much earlier period, when we had a nurse to look after us, she had preferred me, and would march into the room at the sound of screams and, without stopping to enquire what was happening, fix my brother with an accusing eye and say, 'Well, what have you done now?'

This time the situation was reversed. My brother and Noob would walk together, chattering and laughing, while I wandered along, picking grass-heads, on my own. At night Noob would read to my brother by the hour, it seemed, then pop her head in to me with a brief but pleasant 'Goodnight'. She was never unfair, it wasn't in her nature to be, but she was feminine enough to be unable to hide her preference.

My brother and I both knew it; but nothing was ever said. We just accepted it as the luck of the game, as two girls might when one of them gets picked up and the other doesn't. If I thought about it at all I merely considered her choice a little odd. Beyond making use of any natural advantage the situation might offer – quite legitimately in our unwritten and instinctive code – my brother too took no more interest in the fact than I.

Chapter IX
'. . . After They've Seen Paree'

Village life at the time of the first war was still very much as Thomas Hardy has described it in the Wessex novels. Since then the changes have been so fundamental it is hard to realize how comparatively recently they have come.

There was no public transport of any kind. The carrier's cart was virtually the only means of communication between one village and another. Collingbourne Ducis, though, was considered almost a metropolis because it possessed a railway station, admittedly a primitive one, on the little branch line, long since abandoned and overgrown, that then went through to Marlborough. To order our Sunday joint – when we could get it – my mother had to send a postcard to the butcher and await results. Word would eventually filter through that there was a parcel addressed to us at the station and my brother and I would have to trail up the hill to the gaunt little building and search for it among the miscellaneous parcels thrown haphazardly into the dingy, paraffin-smelling lamp room.

Almost everything apart from meat could be bought in the village. There were two shops – or to be more accurate, one and a half. The half was just a cottage presided over by an amiable, red-faced old village body whose stock seemed to consist merely of a few rusty pen-nibs fixed to a card. The other one – appropriately called London House – was a very different affair. As one pressed the brass latch and opened the door one was met by a smell of baking, spice, candle grease, calico, cinnamon, boot polish, coffee, warm wool and cheese – in fact the smell of country shops the world over – and by the figure of Mrs Saunders, tiny and round, like Mrs Tiggy-Winkle, perched on a stool behind the counter from which she could keep the whole village street in sight through a specially devised gap in the window display. Mrs Saunders was as much a part of the village street as the pub or the signpost, and she was so small that she was actually taller when sitting on her stool than when she got off it. This side of the shop was full of such forgotten treasures as Mazawattee Tea and Camp Coffee, showing on the label a splendid, bareheaded Highlander being served outside his tent by a turbaned sepoy; but the counter on the left was festooned with tape, cards of buttons and strange, indecently feminine-looking garments. Here the shopping was done discreetly, in undertones. To my brother and me it was the dull side; of no interest whatsoever.

Our chief reason for venturing out into the village, though, was to visit the farm at the other end of the street. I say venturing because the village boys who hung about, ominously, in the street and on the bridge, made one suddenly aware, for the first time, of the instinctive animal hostility that lies just below the skin between human beings whose speech and clothes are different. In Sutton this problem didn't arise because everyone was roughly the same class – that is to say, of course, the right one. (It never even occurred to me until years later that there might have been people to whom I would have appeared very much as the village boys did to me.)

The boys of the village who whooped past in the lane below on their way home from school, snatching each other's caps and yelling in their rich, West Country voices, were the first of their kind that one had met, as it were, on equal terms. It was only through comparison with them that one began to realize the unnatural softness of one's own sheltered existence, and I felt for them a mixture of fear and admiration. The world of boys is a primitive one where only force commands respect. If a boy from the village came up through the garden to the door with a message he might stand there speechless and apparently respectful until he could hurry back down the path, but one knew that, as soon as the gate clanged behind him, he would burst into ribald and derisive howls. And in a way I agreed with him. By comparison with them – using the basic standards of the school playground, as then unknown to me but already casting its shadow before it – we were a couple of poor things.

Consequently I added to my fear of the dark an unconscious fear of what were still thought of as the lower classes; a fear which I am certain is a great deal more potent, even today, than most people realize.

But we were about to set off on the hazardous trip up the muddy village street, with its stream running down the side, to the farmhouse at the other end. West Farm was a true farmhouse. One went to the back door, through a steaming, pungent yard, picking one's way carefully because the slightest speck of mud on one's boots brought a roar of rage from old Mr Wroth, the farmer. Inside the back door, below a shelf of candles and hand-lamps, stood rows of the family's shoes. The sons were all grown men, now in the army – enormous, larger than life-size, legendary characters they appeared to my brother and me – but when they came home, even if it was straight from France itself, they were never allowed to set foot inside the stone-flagged kitchen without taking their boots off.

The farm was always buzzing with activity. Yard dogs barked insanely at one's approach, rattling their chains with a frantic and obsequious friendliness, pumping engines popped and stuttered unevenly, hobnailed boots clattered on the paved inner courtyard and somebody was generally bawling incomprehensible instructions to somebody else half a mile away who had his back turned. In the cool, dark, lactic-smelling dairy off the kitchen great shallow pans of scalded milk stood on scrubbed trestle tables, because the Wroths were Devonshire by origin and still made vast quantities of clotted cream, even throughout the war. One pushed one's way in humbly, conscious of the fact that this was both an exciting and a rather alarming place, to be met with an agonized cry of 'Wipe your boots, boy! Tst! Dearie, dearie, dearie – what are you thinking of?' as old Mr Wroth, gnarled and twisted as an oak tree, shuffled out of his office. He was a shortish man, of immense breadth and thickness. In fact he must have been almost an exact cube. As with many old people in the village the bones of his legs and hands were badly distorted by arthritis and, like my father, he walked with two sticks. Facially he was not unlike a kind of rustic Bismarck with piercing, light grey eyes that could paralyse a whole tableful of family, guests and strangers at a glance. In fact meals at the farm, taken at a

long table in what was called the schoolroom, were a fright-
ening ordeal. Timid visitors would be reduced to choking fits
while their spoons clattered from nerveless fingers.

When it became impossible for him to walk or ride a horse
Mr Wroth bought a car, the first in the village – a Belsize, with
brass radiator and carriage lamps. It was so high off the
ground that it was a problem to get him in. To do so at least
two of his sons were needed, pushing and straining at his inert
bulk with muffled gasps and grunts, mixed with the kind of
discussion that generally goes with furniture moving – 'Now!
To you! Pull!' 'It's no good, we'll have to get him sideways', etc
– throughout all of which old Mr Wroth, in his hard hat and
gaiters, retained an air of chilling and immobile dignity.

When at last they had levered him into the back – it was an
open car – the only remaining problem was to get him sitting
down. Standing either side, each one would take an arm and
tilt him slightly until, with his great weight beyond their control, he would suddenly collapse backward on to the seat with
an impact that must almost have brought the front wheels off
the ground. There he would sit, swathed in carriage rugs,
calm, monumental, expressionless, his head high above the
level of the windscreen, while he bumped sedately across fields
and cart-tracks, like a Paramount Chieftain or the Emperor
Franz Josef reviewing his troops.

In spite of the overpowering effect of old Mr Wroth himself, the chief impression left in the mind is of a heart-
warming house, whose doors – the back door at any rate –
were never closed; a house in which there were always people
staying or strangers wandering in and out, where in some

room discreetly far away from the ears of Mr Wroth the old wooden horn gramophone was generally playing 'Let the Great Big World Keep Turning' or 'The Bachelor Gay'. Almost everybody came to Salisbury Plain at some time during their army training and a note from the flimsiest acquaintance to say that a son or husband was at Tidworth or Larkhill always brought an open invitation; while returning sons, snatching the occasional 48-hour pass, would turn up unexpectedly, often with a friend, at all hours of the day or night. Nobody was ever turned away and many came repeatedly, without warning. Each time one went there one found new faces; complete strangers, it seemed, whose names nobody bothered to find out; helping with the work or even sleeping, forgotten, on the schoolroom sofa. Games of tennis sprang up, when farm work allowed, or huge picnics by wagonette, Mrs Wroth driving and the men getting out to walk as the horse toiled uphill on the white, gritty lanes to the downs, to be followed, perhaps, by an improvised game of mixed hockey with walking sticks and anything else that would come in handy, because there always seemed to be one or two girls in the party and one had the feeling that, in this atmosphere of sudden arrivals, brief meetings and hurried departures, romance was never very far away.

Looking back on it that household, with its particular atmosphere set against a background of war, as aeroplanes droned over the plain and the guns boomed on the ranges at Bulford and Larkhill, reminds one of an English *Cherry Orchard* or *Uncle Vanya*. But the accent must be on 'English' because nothing could have been less articulate than its inhabitants, especially as they sat round the loaded school-room table under the terrible eye of Mr Wroth. It was a schoolroom charged with unspoken thoughts, with secret glances exchanged while he was otherwise occupied, of friend-ships and romances ripening too quickly in the knowledge that they must end so soon.

Chapter X
My Mother Smokes a Cigarette

Compared with the varied social life of the farm our little world at the Hermitage was quiet indeed. At weekends we would wheel the inevitable bath-chair up the long, curving rise to the station and wait on the deserted, weed-grown platform for the sound of the bell tinkling in the station-master's office and the sight of my father's train puffing into sight from the direction of Andover.

It would come clanking to a halt; one carriage door only would open and very slowly my father would get out, very often with the help of some kind friend made in the twenty minutes or so it took the train to come from the junction – my father was one of those people who are at their best in railway carriages – the flag would wave, the whistle blow, the train rattle away and another twenty-minute friendship had come to an end.

With his bow tie at a slight angle, a pipe in his mouth and his bowler hat exchanged for the doggy peaked cap he wore at weekends he would arrive after a week in Finsbury Square, looking as bronzed and relaxed as though he had just been on a sea voyage.

As I remember it the family atmosphere was better in those months at Collingbourne than it had been in the various cramping villas of the Cornwall Road – certainly better than at Belhaven – and, sadly, much better than it was to become later on. I've no doubt that it suited my father – as to be honest it would many – to be a bachelor for five days in the week and to have the responsibilities of marriage and parenthood for only two.

'There you are, my boy,' he would say, levering himself into one of the shabby armchairs, 'I've brought this for you,' and he would throw us a copy of *The Bystander* or *Tatler* that he had been reading in the train, and we would leaf it eagerly through, ignoring such boring nonsense as the photographs of society beauties, till we came to the Bruce Bairnsfather cartoon of Old Bill, with his boot-button eyes and walrus moustache.

Those weekends must have been very dull for him, with nobody to play cards with and no golf club to visit – only a houseful of women and children. From what I can remember he spent most of his time sketching. It isn't easy to carry a camp stool, a sketching block, water-colour box and brushes when you have to walk with two sticks. Getting my father to the spot of his choice, placing him on the alarmingly inadequate camp stool and supplying his various needs was quite a business. Eventually it would be achieved and we would creep away, possibly relieved to feel that he was securely anchored to one spot and we could safely play somewhere else, as long as it was out of sight and earshot.

Later we would sidle respectfully back as he sat, hunched and concentrated, a sable brush between his teeth. 'May I see?' one would say, peering breathlessly over his shoulder. A false step, threatening to jog his arm or knock the water pot over, would bring an anguished roar of 'Careful boy! What the devil do you think you're playing at!' and we would hastily scatter out of range once more.

We had a very high regard for his painting. Other people's fathers didn't seem to go in for painting. So much the worse for them. We held our breath in awe as he dipped the brush, shook the excess water from it until it had formed a point, then slowly applied the paint with extreme precision and exactness, in small dabs. His drawing, particularly of buildings, was meticulously careful, as one would expect an architect's to be, and the paint was for the most part very dry, with few free washes. In short it was a style in the good Victorian water-colourist's tradition, though of course we knew nothing of such things at the time. We were full of admiration for the fact that he painted every leaf and every brick, so neatly and without smudging, as we always did. Later, in more sophisticated times, it was this quality of fussy neatness that made me dismiss his sketches with slight embarrassment. It was much later again that, coming across one he did of the Hermitage, I found in it a kind of stiff charm and honesty that had completely escaped me before. It makes one wonder how objective one's judgements ever are.

It was during our stay at Collingbourne that I can remember my parents taking part in a family joke. This may not have been nearly as remarkable as my memory of it seems to be. Neither was a particularly solemn sort of person, but I suspect that they didn't laugh at the same things. In later days, while waiting for the cab to take him to the golf club on Saturday mornings, my father would sometimes indulge in bursts of high spirits much more in tune with us children than with his wife; but yet again, if in the course of the fun a harmless paper dart floated close to his head his mood would suddenly change and he would bellow: 'Look out what you're doing, can't you, boy! You nearly had my eye out.'

You never quite knew. It was best to be careful. But I can't remember any outbursts at Collingbourne. It was an idyllic time. Looking back, one is always trying to reinterpret the memories of a child by the light of one's later knowledge. One is always looking for a significance beyond the understanding of early days.

One evening, under the heady influence of life at the farm, with the gramophone playing and old Mr Wroth safely out of the way, my mother was prevailed upon to smoke a cigarette. I don't know what the exact circumstances would have been, because of course I was at the other end of the village, back at the Hermitage, in bed. But news of it was spread, presumably by herself.

Pictures of women actually holding cigarettes were beginning to appear in newspapers and periodicals. It was very 'emancipated'. My father had previously let it be known that if ever his wife took to smoking he would grow a beard in revenge.

The next Friday evening, when we went up to meet him at the station, he appeared at the carriage window, looking rather like a French murderer, with a large false beard and moustache; to the great satisfaction of a carriageful of soldiers, who, in the space of the twenty-minute run, had been let into the joke.

It was one of the few occasions that I can remember when both of my parents laughed at the same time.

Chapter XI
A Heavenly Visitant

One bright winter day, when my brother and I were playing in the Hermitage garden during our mid-morning break from lessons, an Avro 504K training plane circled low over the village several times; so low that we paused in our game, convinced as always that it was our house and no other that the pilot was diving on.

After it had come round a second time – 'only just missing the chimneys, honestly!' as we afterwards said, with more enthusiasm than accuracy – my brother said, 'He's looking for somewhere to land. He's coming down.'

My brother was over two years older than I. He knew about such things.

It was our perpetual dream that one day an aeroplane would actually make a forced landing, or even crash, in front of our very eyes. Many times when out on our walks with Noob one of the SE5s or Bristol Fighters from Upavon would suddenly swoop down so low that its undercarriage almost brushed the tops of the bushes – 'hedge-hopping' as it was called – perhaps disappearing in a sudden silence behind a rise in the ground or a clump of trees, while with shrill cries we would urge poor Noob into a reluctant trot, convinced that this time the miracle had happened; only to see it zoom away again into the distance, to be followed seconds later by the renewed but rapidly dwindling sound of its engine.

On this occasion, though we listened expectantly enough, there was only silence. The significance was not lost upon us. We stared at each other hopefully.

At this moment Noob came to call us in again. She stood outside the back door, her long, pointed nose glistening pinkly in the cold air. 'Come along, lads!' she called.

She had a particular way of doing this, musically and always in the same cadence, like the familiar chime of the clock. Secretly it rather embarrassed us.

'Come along, lads!' she repeated.

This time we rushed up and clamoured round her.

'There's an aeroplane!' we said.

'It must have come down,' we yelled.

'It came so low you could actually see the pilot,' we screamed.

'It almost touched the roof,' we bellowed.

'It did,' we roared, almost beside ourselves. 'It did, Noob, honestly it did.'

And this time it was really true. Our prayers were answered and the miracle had happened. News soon flashed round the village that an aeroplane had crashed in the field next to the school playground. By great good luck my father had not gone back to London that week. Somehow he managed to be one of the first to arrive at the spot – I suspect he was as avid for outside excitement as we were – and found a man in the fur-helmeted flying kit of the period, standing erect before the crumpled machine, smoking a cigarette.

'Alone I did it,' the young man said, waving a dismissive hand in the direction of the wreckage.

Engine trouble at a very low altitude had given him little choice of landing place. He managed to pick the one field that looked reasonably flat, but as he came in his tail skid caught the telegraph wires – fortunately as it happened – pulling him round and causing him to land one wing down.

The undercarriage buckled, ploughing through the turf, and the plane skidded to a stop, tail in the air, a few yards short of the school playground. If he had landed normally, he told my father, he would certainly have overshot – possibly with disastrous results.

My father, always at his best when making a new acquaintance, especially one as unusual as this, immediately offered all the hospitality that the Hermitage could muster for as long as it might be necessary, regardless of the domestic difficulties, which were not in any case his, and we all trooped back through the village, at my father's slow pace, with the erect figure in the flying suit beside him.

It was a magical day. My brother and I sat spellbound, too awed to speak, while my father chatted freely to the newcomer and seemed to enjoy his company almost as much as we did. It was a revelation. We had never admired our father so much.

Looking back I don't find my father's reactions nearly so surprising. In spite of his romantic appearance he was one of those men who are soon bored by the company of women. He had no natural taste for their interests. Here was a young man – an extremely masculine young man – literally dropping from the skies to provide him with a new acquaintance, always a stimulus in itself, and someone who could probably talk sport and might even play cards. It was a completely unlooked-for piece of luck.

Even Noob came under the visitor's spell. Whenever he looked in her direction her china blue eyes would flutter and her long, spinster's nose seemed to quiver with delighted embarrassment. He told us his name – but everyone called him 'Mac', he said; so 'Mac' he became and Mac he shall be. Just to write that name or say it to myself now, many decades later, brings back to the surface a mixture of sensations and prejudices so complex that three-quarters of a lifetime has not yet sorted them out.

'Mac'. It has a period ring to it. Is anybody called – simply – 'Mac' now? It was a first war name. And there was a first war face. So many young men, peering out of silver photograph frames or from faded family albums, who never got beyond the stage of sleek, brushed-back hair cut short and parted at the side, generally with a little clipped toothbrush moustache to add a touch of masculine authority – the heroes of the Royal Flying Corps – Bishop, Ball, MacCudden, or Wilfred Owen, the poet of the trenches. Mac looked something between them all, though he had no moustache. He had jet-black wavy hair, which he did his best to plaster back in the proper fashion and extremely piercing, potent grey eyes. Tall and stiff-backed, he spoke in the tight-lipped, staccato manner of the time and he seemed charged with a masculinity that crackled like static electricity.

He stayed the whole day, until the breakdown crew from Upavon came in the evening to collect him and salvage the crashed plane. It was a never-to-be-forgotten day for all of us, as it turned out, but at the time I think it was my brother and I who cherished it most. We were exalted. We felt as the Jews must have done; we were the chosen among all those other families who had not had an airman staying for the day.

A few days later, as we were playing in the garden again, a small sound gradually gathered itself into a roar and a plane dived right down, quite unmistakably over our house and no other. Once again, it was 'so low that it almost hit the chimney', as we repeated a hundred times, only this time with more truth, and one could actually recognize Mac in the cockpit, in his goggles.

More wonderful still he waved. To us – my brother and me, little khaki-clad dots standing on the Hermitage lawn. In a roar of noise he banked round over the village, swerved away, then came back again, diving over us once more and giving the thumbs-up sign.

Providence could hardly have done more for us. If an angel in all the panoply of light had settled on the Hermitage roof we couldn't have felt more distinguished.

During that day he spent at the Hermitage a link had been forged. How it came about I honestly don't know, but it was one which was to have a strong but not easily defined effect upon all of us; though each was to be influenced in a different way.

Chapter XII
Down to Earth

The war was over. We were back once more in the Cornwall Road. Financially precarious as ever, we were now installed – by courtesy of my grandfather – in Melton, the red-brick and roughcast counterpart of the unsightly Belhaven, where Pix and Uncle Ath still lived.

There had been a time when – understandably one now feels – my grandfather had hung back and shown some reluctance to come to our rescue. He had temporarily withdrawn his all-too-necessary support for some reason, as a mark of disfavour towards my father who, even as a child, I knew he did not like. There were mutterings between my parents which died with obvious suddenness as one came into the room. My mother was distressed. My father relapsed into his usual protective dyspepsia. While maintaining an attitude of respect towards my grandfather in front of his sons, he somehow managed to convey the impression that he thought his father-in-law could have done more for us if he'd really wanted to.

Needless to say, my grandfather's wealth was no match for the silent blackmail of his impecunious dependants. Melton, in all its suburban splendour, was eventually ours. Once more the chauffeur-driven Armstrong Siddeley could be seen outside our privet hedge and small, green front gate, bestowing on us all a distinction that must have been about our only tangible asset, and the stage was set for the remaining brief four years or so of our life as a family unit.

In passing I should say that I think this whole question of money, or the lack of it, is one which affects children much more than many people realize. It was never openly discussed, as far as I can remember, yet a feeling of insecurity certainly came through to us in some indefinable way. Children, like dogs, are extremely susceptible to an emotional climate. If anyone had told me that my father had only five pounds in the world it would have meant nothing to me – indeed five pounds would probably have seemed to me like wealth – yet the anxiety that sometimes floated about the house like a smell of drains was something we absorbed and understood in some deep, primitive way.

So there we were, in those far-off days just after the first war, the four of us and the scarcely existent but essential Lizzie. It was now that a hardly perceptible change came over the household; one that crept up unnoticed and was only perceived in retrospect. It changed its sex.

In our earliest days we had had a nurse, as all the other children in the Cornwall Road did, and afterwards, in the idyllic days of Collingbourne and the Hermitage there had been Noob. In those shamefully soft and happy times, if one fell and hurt oneself feminine hands would bear one up and bring comfort. Now that was all over. Noob departed and, much older than the proper starting age and therefore suspect from the beginning, we were to go to the local preparatory school, chiefly noted for having supplied a number of illustrious amateurs to the Surrey cricket team.

For some time the prospect of school had been casting a shadow before it; but now that the dreaded day was near there was at least one compensation: it was more than a mile away, down the privet- and laurel-lined suburban roads of Sutton; too far for us to walk each day; so we were given our first bicycles. (My brother, being older, had one with Sturmey-Archer three-speed gears while mine had nothing; but I've more or less got over that now.)

The impact of a large and highly competitive boys' school on those as totally unprepared as we were was considerable and would, one hopes, be almost impossible now. Even at this length of time the sound of that babel of voices as one approached, late as usual, down the Mulgrave Road, rings ominously in my ears. And if the bell went as one was still trying to force one's bike into an already bursting bicycle shed, the clamour would suddenly stop and, worse still, one would be left stranded, a conspicuous figure on the empty tarmac, surrounded by panic-inducing emptiness and silence – late! Afterwards the breathless squeeze into Prayers – carbolic wax and an out-of-tune piano – the longed-for inconspicuousness, the grim prospect of school dinner and worst of all, looming sensibly nearer every moment, inevitable, unavoidable, the awful school lavatories.

But even more influential in our lives was the reappearance of Mac. After the war he joined one of the first companies hoping to run an air passenger service between London and Paris, and because the London end of the trip had lately been moved from Hounslow aerodrome to the larger, more modern one at Croydon, and the Cornwall Road was not many miles away, he became, by mutual consent, our lodger.

His was the all-pervading influence that somehow, by the sheer strength of his personality, coloured all our lives. He was the fulcrum, the point of balance, between our early, childish days and what was to come. The advent of Mac, as I say, changed our household. The suburbia of popular legend is a place peopled by a race of identikit men, each wearing a bowler hat and carrying a briefcase and umbrella. If it was ever true, which I doubt, it certainly did not apply to the household at Melton. My father, admittedly, wore a bowler hat, which my mother brushed daily with a specially curved brush, kept in the mock-antique oak hat cupboard in the hall – the particular squeak made by the door as she slammed it shut afterwards has survived in my memory to this moment – but it was a bowler hat whose curly brim and jaunty angle somehow conveyed the impression of a slight wink.

After my father's cab had clattered away towards Sutton

station Mac would leave the house with a splutter and a roar on the Norton motor bike that my brother and I regarded with such awe, to ride the few miles to Croydon, perhaps returning to the Cornwall Road and one of Lizzie's famed steak-and-kidney puds that evening after lunching in Paris.

At other times he would be missing for weeks or even months on some flying mission much farther afield; then the feeling of tension that his powerful personality generated would gradually evaporate and it was safe to play feeble, childish games again. For Mac was an apostle of toughness and all the manly virtues – that adjective that nowadays seems to require inverted commas. Immediately after leaving school he had been shipped off to Canada, alone, to find his own salvation. 'When my father died,' he would say, 'he left me the whole wide world to work in.'

His salvation was the war. Returning with the Canadian expeditionary force he soon transferred to the Flying Corps and the training school at Upavon, where we found him.

He had that particular brand of cynicism that was endemic at the time. Only a fool does a disinterested act for anyone else. Look after number one. The world's a rough, tough place; to hold your own you've got to be rougher and tougher than the next man – and toughness begins at school.

Cycling back home with one's satchel on one's back, a feeling of dread would strike one in the stomach at the sight of that Norton outside the front gate.

'Well, and what have you been up to at school today?' he would say, fixing the victim of the moment with his cold, glinting eye.

'Oh, nothing much.'

'No fights?'

'No.'

'Absolutely sure? I can't believe it. I should have thought you'd have been the terror of the playground.'

Sometimes he would just stand there and say, 'Hit me. Go on, punch me as hard as you can.'

Totally uncombative by nature, one feebly complied.

'Harder. Go on, harder. That wouldn't hurt a fly.' Then, when one had failed again – 'Hasn't anyone ever shown you the proper way to clench your fist? Come here.'

He once came with us on a summer holiday, to Paignton, and decided he would teach my brother and me to swim. We knew, of course, what would happen; and it did. For a few moments he held us up, then just let go. We screamed loudly enough to attract a great deal of attention and sank straight to the bottom; to be hauled out gasping and spluttering by my mother.

Mac was disgusted; while our secret resentment was longer lasting. Twenty years later my brother taught himself to swim, in secret; I still can't.

This whole question of physical toughness is one that often bothers the young in their school days; and of course it is peculiar to one sex only. Many boys, without doubt, go through school obsessed with fears of inadequacy and a lack of sheer physical courage which must at all costs be hidden from the world. The lesser suburban Rugby clubs must be full of those secretly trying to prove their manhood to themselves. This is one of the few private phobias that women don't have o bother about – at least until after marriage.

But if Mac was a product of his age in his attitude to the world in general he was, too, in many other ways. His manner of speaking in clipped, staccato bursts, hardly moving his lips, was very much of the period; so was his brand of mocking, dead-pan humour, which was often baffling to a ten-year-old because it was never possible to tell from his expression which were jokes and which were not.

One day, in the middle of breakfast, he turned to my mother in his most unsmiling manner and said: 'Norah dear, I do wish you wouldn't have sausages on any day but Sunday. It's so confusing. You know how I always start praying after sausages.'

When my brother and I laughed, pretty sure that this was a joke, he turned his steely eye round on us.

'Never poke fun at religion, my boy. Surely your Uncle Ath has told you that?'

You couldn't win.

He pretended, too, a great erotic interest in poor, plain, almost anonymous Lizzie. Hearing her go upstairs to her bedroom in its particular brand of limbo he would half rise from his chair, as though impelled by some irresistible force and turn to my mother.

'She's gone up. May I go, dear?'

My mother, half-amused, yet embarrassed for our sakes, would try to shut him up.

'Oh Norah, just this once. Just this once, dear. Go on, be a sport.'

The actual, physical difference between the sexes had, at

this period of my life, quite escaped my notice, so the implied joke was lost on me; yet even so one sensed that this was a taboo subject and one therefore suffered the humiliation, so much a part of childhood, of a joke from which one is excluded.

Not all his jokes were beyond us. Normally the water was heated by the old-fashioned kitchen range, but in the scullery was the ancient, gas-fired contrivance, previously mentioned, known as a Potterton Boiler, which was called into use only in emergencies. But Mac affected a great fastidiousness. When it was lighted for him he would say, with a slightly reproving expression, 'Oh Norah dear, you know I never bathe in Potterton-heated water.'

Looking back one wonders what in the world the rest of the Cornwall Road made of our strange ménage – and it was to become progressively stranger. One wonders, too, what could have been the true relationships and undercurrents in this ill-assorted trio? What, for instance, between Mac and my father. Memory tells me that, for the most part, it was very good. They shared many interests – sport of all kinds, a love of playing cards for money and a bland indifference to the concerns of the female sex, at any rate on a domestic level. Mac was an up-to-date version of that eighteenth-century man of adventure, the corsair. As a bachelor with no family ties of any kind he was free to go anywhere and do anything, to indulge in amorous adventures all over the world and, from scraps of memory recaptured in later years, undoubtedly did; but within the confines of Melton one assumes that he restricted himself merely to the masculine qualities of charm and self-interest.

In retrospect one sees him as a symbol of the gathering tensions of the household – a knotting of the muscles against a blow to come. Once he took a job in Peking, teaching the Chinese to fly and helping them to form an air force. For many months the tensions relaxed until news came that he was returning by the newly opened trans-Siberian railway. For several weeks the dining-room mirror at Melton was decorated with laconic cables: 'Irkutsk OK' and 'Omsk all merry and bright'.

Then, one day when we were playing at the bottom of the garden, we heard the portentous sound of the Norton coming to a halt outside the front gate.

'Well, and what mischief have you been getting up to while I was away?'

'Oh, nothing much.'

'What – no mischief at all? No fights? I don't believe you.'

And one would creep away, crushed once again by one's own inadequacy and full of uncontrollable and disturbing emotions, too strong to be understood, but certain of one thing – the occupation had begun again.

Chapter XIII
My Father's Day

In all the years of my childhood I can never once remembe
my father being in time for breakfast. When we had all fin
ished and the table was littered with dirty plates and empt
cups the slow slip-slop of his dragging feet would sound o
the stairs, the door would open and my father, steadying him
self with a hand on the dining-room sideboard, would flin
his two sticks into an armchair and with a look of martyrdon
that forestalled any adverse criticism, lower himself slowl
into his chair. If there was a bill waiting beside his plate i
would be greeted by a deep groan and he would pass his han
slowly over his bronzed, unfurrowed brow. If it was from hi
bookmaker he would seize the first opportunity to open it i

secret, below the level of the table, suppressing his facial reaction to a brief spasm of pain.

Through the wall, in Belhaven, a similar scene had been enacted, only a little earlier. It was clearly a characteristic of my father's family that nobody came down at the right time in the mornings, but whereas my father entered the room in a state of defiant self-pity, Uncle Ath would come in shaking his head and muttering, 'Here's a time to come down to breakfast!' It didn't stop him coming down at exactly the same time the next day – or the day after, and the day after that. The other difference was that in Belhaven there were no bookmaker's bills.

Once seated in his chair my father would look up and, with a cry of pain, clap a hand over his eyes. 'Oh, I'm blinded, I'm blinded. Quick, boy!' My mother, clearing away the plates, would say in an ordinary, conversational tone: 'One of you boys just pull the curtain for your father, would you?'

It was a kind of ritual, not unlike the summer solstice at Stonehenge. Presumably the sun rose at roughly the same time and place each day, allowing for seasonal variations. Our dining-room table and my father's place at it being fixed, it should have been possible to work out exactly in advance the point at which the sun's rays would strike the sacrificial object – my father's head.

It was never done. Perhaps, in our different ways, we all enjoyed this piece of family drama.

My brother, jumping up, would pull a curtain: 'There, now's that, Dad?'

'No, no, you stupid boy – not that one' – with more histrionic groans.

'Well this? Or this? Is that better?'

It was a bay window with a number of curtains. You could keep it up for quite a long time.

My father's other popular domestic performance was reserved for meals later in the day. He had a unique talent for finding pieces of grit in salad. Chewing away happily like the rest of us, he would utter a sudden cry and freeze, in apparent agony, clasping his cheek with both hands.

We would all stop eating and watch, fascinated, while his eyes gradually opened again and he glared at my mother in dumb reproach. It was as though yet another attempt had been made on his life and the fault was somehow hers. As always his reaction was so extreme that one tended to disbelief; but sensing this, and just to prove our callousness, my father would silently eject from his mouth several small pieces of rock or shrapnel which fell on to his plate with an audible tinkle. Then, still without speech but with a sigh of resignation, he would go on eating.

Breakfast over, there would be a brief walk in the garden, supported by his two sticks, to select a rose for his buttonhole. This was an extremely important moment to my father. 'How is it old Connie always manages to have a rose every day? How does he do it?' he would report his friends as having said. Whether or not they really did, one couldn't tell, but at least it was an indication of what he would like them to have said.

The rose selected, he would place it in the small metal container, like half a pencil case, the bottom filled with water from the kitchen tap, which stuck through the lapel of his overcoat. By this time the cab would be waiting at the front gate, and a cry of 'Cab's here' would come from everyone, while my father remained outwardly unruffled. But once the cab had finally rattled away down the Worcester Road in the direction of Sutton station a great calm would settle over the household; a calm which, I suppose, has settled over all suburban streets at this time of day for many generations.

Meanwhile my father, freed from the constraints of his family, had become a different man. Once in the London Bridge train – a First Class compartment, of course – and among his little band of daily intimates, known as the Cronies, he left behind the anxieties and oppressions of domestic life and became truly himself.

'Hullo,' they'd shout, 'here he is – the great man himself.'

'Any room for a little 'un?'

'Here – budge up there. Make room for old Connie.'

If any stranger, particularly a woman, was foolhardy enough to try to break in on them there was a trick you could play of putting your foot against the handle – being careful to keep your leg below the level of the window.

'I'm sorry, madam, I think it must be locked. Plenty of room next door.'

Once the train was in motion they would get down to the serious business of the day.

'Well now,' somebody would begin, 'what does everyone say to a little game of cards, eh?'

'Cards? Cards? What are they?'

'You'll have to teach me. I don't know how to play.'

The journey from Sutton to London Bridge took not more

than about half an hour; but for my father it must surely have been the happiest part of the day, because here, among the Cronies, he was spiritually at home.

At this long distance one sees them as a shadowy band. For some reason one pictures them always in straw hats; essentially male and essentially jolly; like something out of *Three Men in a Boat*. Jollity, as such, was a purely masculine state. Women – or at any rate ladies – were never actually jolly, though they might be happy or even high-spirited, in moderation, and, if nature had been kind to them, witty; but jollity of the exuberant, rib-tickling kind was too nearly allied to that great bastion of male supremacy, the Smoking Room. Even the most innocuous joke would bring a wink and a 'Hey, there, ladies present, old chap': not, surely, to preserve those delicate ears which, one hopes, were never quite as delicate as they were thought to be, but to maintain the vast chasm that still separated the sexes. When women were safely protected from absolutely everything, male supremacy had reached its peak.

But such arguments were foreign to the Cronies. They were a simple, happy bunch, not unlike elderly schoolboys in spirit. There was Mr Pothecary – 'Old Potts' – a florid bachelor accountant; 'Old Roly Blades', later, as Sir Rowland, to become a Lord Mayor of London; and somebody always referred to as 'Nicholas-Tickle-us' – I never knew his real name but presume he was a Mr Nicholas, as Christian names were never used, even among these intimate friends of long standing. Greatest Crony of all, though, was Mr Flower, known – of course – as 'Old Blossom'. He was my father's special friend.

One would say he was rather handsome, in a gentle, woe-begone way, with mild blue eyes behind his pince-nez, set at a rakish slant and secured by a light chain to a spring device on his lapel, which, at a slight tug, would suddenly wind them in – fascinating! – while a permanent, hand-rolled cigarette, emerging from his drooping, Lord Balfour-type moustache, stuck to his top lip and wobbled when he talked. My father had a deep respect for him because he was a good golfer, with a single-figure handicap, and was said to have made a hundred break at billiards; but what irresistibly drew my father to him, and indeed gave him an automatic entrée into our more intimate circle, was the fact that he had gone bankrupt and been hammered from the Stock Exchange.

My father had a natural affinity with all bankrupts. If he didn't seek them out they sought him. He could smell one in a heap of solvent men as a pig smells truffles. And some, too, who were financially normal when he befriended them, at once became bankrupt, as though simply to conform. For years we used to hear about a Portuguese millionaire for whom my father designed a big, cut-price store in London, whose give-away wrapping paper and shopping bags with their slogan 'Why does Portella sell so cheaply?' all over them we found a bit embarrassing.

We were none of us surprised by the answer to his rhetorical question.

Like many, from the White Knight onward, my father was particularly susceptible to all begetters of Schemes and Inventions. Ever hopeful, he would come back in the evening full of some new venture that would transform all our lives and solve our problems 'at a stroke'. The last I can remember was a company for marketing a device by which fat men could put on their boots. Our problems remained unsolved.

But my father's train is nearing London Bridge. Familiar signs through the carriage window warn the Cronies that time is running short.

'Better make that the last, I suppose,' says my father. 'Let's see, how much do I owe you?'

'Oh, never mind that now. We can settle up tonight, at Old Blossom's place.'

'What, is it cards again tonight, then?'

'Oh no, not cards. Not at Old Blossom's. He doesn't allow cards – not Old Blossom – do you, old chap? Well, not for money, anyhow.'

And they would break up and go their separate ways. For my father this meant another cab ride, over London Bridge, to his office in Finsbury Square, lunch and a cigar at Frascati's and later – not so very much later – the return cab drive to London Bridge and finally up the Worcester Road from Sutton station.

Of that part – not a large part – of my father's day actually spent in his office we knew nothing except, of course, through his eyes. There were the new and influential clients who demanded to see him, personally, and not his partner, and there was Miss Cochrane.

She was the staff and always, one was intended to infer, on my father's side in any discussion with his partner. Her name cropped up so repeatedly in all my father's office anecdotes that my mother was driven to the kind of tepid curiosity that all women feel about the other women who have dealings, however superficial, with their husbands. My vision of her is of a large, very pale young woman, with nearly colourless fair hair and a white blouse tucked into a belt.

But then again, on second thoughts, I'm not too sure that I ever actually saw her.

The sound of my father's cab approaching was one of those daily domestic signals by which most families live. It created no shock-wave of apprehension, like the approach of Mac's motor cycle, but then again it signalled the end of the more relaxed part of the day, when tennis balls could be retrieved from flowerbeds without even a first, cautious glance to see if anybody was looking.

After tea, if it was summer, he would sit for hours among the roses and crazy paving, in a deckchair, sucking the ring on the end of his silver pencil, withdrawn, aloof – mentally gardening. At these times my brother or I, apparently safe in the knowledge that we were behind his back and out of vision, would venture a foot on the sacred earth, only to hear his sudden roar as some special sense, apparently located in the back of his neck, told him to turn round at exactly the wrong moment.

'Here, here! What the devil are you up to, boy? You'll smash down my roses!'

He had a very strong sense of possession; these were always 'his' roses, or it was 'his' lawn or 'his' pergola. We forbore to tell him we were merely recovering 'our' ball.

After an early supper a cab would again come to the front gate to take him the half mile or so to Old Blossom's house in the York Road, returning there to bring him home, for the last ride of the day, at about midnight.

(This raises the question in one's mind: when, if ever, did the cabbies sleep? Memory seems to suggest that they merely dozed on their boxes between, and sometimes during, trips.)

The next morning, as we heard the slow, familiar sound of his approach, we would all know in our hearts that our family morale for the day would largely depend on what sort of cards he had held the night before; and in retrospect my father seems to have been the unluckiest of players.

As the two walking-sticks crashed into the armchair he would lever himself painfully into his seat and stare gloomily at his plate.

'That whisky of Old Blossom's is the filthiest muck you ever tasted. I can't think where in the world he gets the stuff.'

'I wish you'd said you didn't want any breakfast, Steph dear,' my mother would answer. 'I would have told Lizzie not to bother.'

It was at this point that, looking up to make some general reply, my father would again be struck by the sacrificial shaft. There would be the sudden cry, the arm flung up, shielding the delicate mechanism of the eye as from a mortal blow, the scramble of his sons to the window.

'This one? Is that right?'

'How's that, Dad?'

'No, no, you stupid boy. Not that one. Oh quick – I'm blinded, I'm blinded!'

Shaking her head silently at the waste my mother would take his uneaten breakfast out and throw it in the dustbin.

Chapter XIV
On Not Going to School

Mac was not always with us. During his periods abroad we could safely revert to our pre-Mac softness. This generally took the form of persuading our unfortunate mother not to send us to school. We were so successful in this that for long periods we hardly went at all. When we did go, our appearance created more surprise and interest than anyone else's absence.

My own dislike of school was obsessive and illogical. Even now, when children confess that they quite enjoy it, I refuse to believe them. Why did I dislike it all so intensely? I really don't know. I was never bullied or ill-treated by other boys – somehow I wasn't the type who is. I was average at games; I was above average at work. This, really, was the trouble. At a boys' school it is the talented player of games who is the admired figure both by the other boys and the staff – in this as in many other things the difference is negligible – while prowess in class is less, if at all, admired.

And in this I was totally at one with all the others. I, too, liked and admired – indeed greatly envied – those jaunty characters who were heroes on the cricket field and who had a normal, healthy disregard for work.

Yet I couldn't copy them. Some demon within me, whose presence I resented, forced me to pore over my hated homework and do it to the best of my ability. It was certainly not a desire to excel; to me, as to the others, excellence was not measured in the classroom.

My mother became concerned and consulted the head-master. An ex-county cricketer himself, he fully agreed that my whole attitude, though not actually culpable, was certainly not to be encouraged. On Saturday mornings it was his cus-tom to go into each classroom to distribute the weekly 'cards' with their form placing. It was a tense moment. We all sat straight and held our breath. He had a 'presence'; in fact he was an older version of Mac. Holding the pause as long as he could, for maximum effect, he would look round the class with his awful eye until it lighted on me. He would then hang his head in mock-grief, shaking it slowly from side to side.

'Poor old Constanduros,' he would say, enjoying his own performance. 'Poor old Constanduros' . . . pause . . . 'Top again!' And he would flip the card on to my desk, amid a roar of sycophantic laughter from the class, while I would once again suffer the humiliation of my success.

Sometimes, of course, our reasons for not going to school were genuine enough. We were subject to the same crop of minor ailments as anyone else. Those were indeed days to be remembered.

I believe one of the chief pleasures of childhood is being ill. Not very ill, of course, but just slightly. Few things in later life can equal the deep and secret happiness of lying in bed while the thermometer is being read; to be told, in the special voice used for invalids, 'You'd better stay there today, anyway.' In that glorious moment even school, grown suddenly inaccessible, becomes a pleasant place to remember, full of fun and friendliness. A moment before, the thermometer still under one's tongue, fate hung in the balance, while the sound of the school bell or the Jeyes Fluid smell of early morning class-rooms in the imagination brought a spasm of foreboding to the pit of the stomach.

Until the thermometer was actually read there was always the possibility that one was 'just making it up'. Clearly no grown-up was going to take one's word for it and, to be honest, one wasn't too sure oneself. Then, suddenly, with science on one's side in the shape of the thermometer – what bliss! Illness at last! Perhaps the *Boy's Own Paper*, *Chums* or *All Sports* brought home from a shopping expedition in Sutton High Street; or even, highest award of all, rarely bestowed, a coal fire in the bedroom and a pot of Brand's chicken jelly. Even as one lay there, important and privileged, one knew inwardly that nothing would ever again equal the first morning; that by evening the bedclothes would be hot and untidy, the bed full of crumbs, one's eyes and mind jaded with reading and that the voices from the garden would sound enviably free and happy. Worse still, one's hour of personal glory would have passed. The sweet-sounding 'Anything else I can get you, dear?' would have changed to 'Was that you ringing again?' and finally, 'I wish I'd counted how many times I've run up and down these stairs since this morning!' The next day, per-haps, the thermometer reading would simply bring a brisk – 'Oh well, I think you can get up after lunch.' That was the end. From that moment one lay there on sufferance, a mere nuisance, able to fetch things for oneself, to slink downstairs later, pale and wobbly-legged, and revert glumly to one's old, inconspicuous place in the scheme of things.

But this good fortune seldom came my way; it was reserved for my brother. A beneficent providence had given him a tendency to bronchitis which, apart from bestowing on him an enviable distinction, kept him in bed for long periods in the winter. The gods had not been so kind to me. Apart from a little hay-fever in the summer I could boast of nothing. I can remember to this day the sense of injustice as my mother, her hand on his forehead, said those fateful words: 'Just a moment, dear. Stay there and I'll get the thermometer.' Afterwards there he would lie, hardly bothering to hide the look of smug satisfaction, while my mother went to fetch the steam kettle – a device with a long, proboscis-like spout which sat on a gas ring in his bedroom, belching out vaporized Friar's Balsam – and Gamage's catalogue for him to look at.

Nursing a sense of injustice I would sit in silence at the breakfast table – my father, of course, would not be down yet – doing my best to radiate gloom and ill health. Africans, it is said, can will themselves dead in quite a short time; children can will themselves sick even quicker. Wretched with apprehension at the prospect of the day ahead I would sit there in silence until my mother, unable to bear it any longer, would weaken.

'Oh, very well,' she would sigh, 'I suppose you'd better stay at home today and keep him company. But only today, mind!'

The whole world was suddenly a different place. Joy! Bliss! Reprieve!

Then, inevitably, the reaction. Guilt. Remorse. What had I

done to my mother? But I did feel sick, I would reassure myself. Honestly I did. Well, slightly anyway.

Stifling my conscience without too much difficulty I would go bounding back upstairs to the bedroom.

As I say, there was something wonderful about those ill-gotten and undeserved days away from school; days when, without actually admitting it to each other, we slipped back into a pre-Mac, pre-school world of childhood. My brother, from the vantage point of his bed, would demand things to be brought from the nursery cupboard downstairs. Vast armies of lead soldiers would range across the bedroom floor again – to be ground to extinction later by Lizzie, bringing the invalid's steamed fish (she had the most lethal feet of anyone I have known) – or elaborate palaces made of postcards would rise, tottering, to enormous heights. This was my speciality. We had a large collection of picture postcards, mostly of military subjects, and these I would build into skyscrapers, storey by storey, until they were so high that one had to stand on a chair, selecting each card individually for its weight and strength, then gradually placing it, with breath held and hand steadied, while the whole structure rocked several inches out of the perpendicular with the additional weight.

The early stages of building were rather boring, though care had to be used in selecting strong cards at the bottom; photographs I remember, with a glazed surface, had a tendency to curl and buckle if used on the side facing the gas fire; but when one had got past the ten-storey mark and the chair was necessary, tension rose and the placing of each card could take several agonizing minutes – to be greeted with an audible expelled gasp of relief if the swaying building recovered itself or with shouts of rage if, as frequently happened, some blundering grown-up, carrying a tray, ignorant and insensitive to what was going on, opened the door suddenly and caused a slight current of air which would bring the whole delicate affair crashing to the ground.

The mornings, then, were pure bliss; but as the day wore on and the light began to fade, thoughts of the following morning and school would inevitably creep back. Fatigue would render the invalid less companionable. The games that had been the delight of the morning were now just a mess that had to be cleared up from the floor and put back into the right boxes. With the switching on of the electric light and the drawing of the curtains came the time for temperatures to rise on the one hand and on the other for spirits to drop.

The next morning, one knew, would bring no further reprieve. Whatever my brother's temperature might be I would be condemned to set off down the Cornwall Road on my bicycle, the pink cap of servitude on my head and the satchel full of forgotten homework bumping against my back.

My mother, of course, had the power over us to say whether or not we were fit to go to school. It seemed to me at the time that that power was absolute, and that the wielding of it was a mere matter of saying a few words. It was only much later, when I was in her own position, that I realized the greater, more damaging power, lies with the child.

Yet, to be absolutely honest, did I not realize it at the time? I fear that, somewhere in my subconscious mind, after the manner of children, I did.

Chapter XV
A Liberal Education

After a while my unfortunate parents gave up all pretence of sending us to school. For a time the garden of Melton rang with our happy cries and the tennis lawn was permanently ringed with tyre marks.

But such a blissful state couldn't last long. It was decided that we were to have a tutor. I don't know whose idea it was and it sounds on the face of it rather grand. The truth, I suspect, is that it was an economy measure. Unemployment was already rising and there must have been a large number of adequately educated young men with no particular qualifications of any sort, whose last hope was to find some gullible family like ours who would feed them in return for a few hours of boredom spent teaching elementary French and arithmetic to their sub-normal children. That is how the situation must have appeared from the tutor's end; from the employer's it was very different.

My parents started out with high hopes for their new scheme. Two sons educated for the price of one must have seemed an attractive proposition to my father. Added to which he no doubt looked forward to the prospect of some male company in the house, because the change was made during one of Mac's more prolonged absences abroad. But they were soon to discover the apparently fundamental truth that nobody undertakes the job of resident tutor, at any rate to a household such as ours was in the Cornwall Road, unless there is something slightly strange about him.

Our first applicant was a young man recently down from a university with the reassuring Scottish name of Cameron. I don't know why the fact of being a Scot should have given such an impression of solid dependability to my parents, but I'm sure that it did.

His appearance, when at last he came, was not at all what we were expecting. Instead of the rugged Celt that we all visualized, he turned out to be very small, dark and dapper; in fact not so much Gaelic as Gallic. His manners were impeccable. He would spring lightly to his feet, with a winning smile, as soon as my mother entered the room. This was so unlike the treatment she was used to that she was charmed.

The first slight shock came at Christmas, when he spent the whole of one evening walking up and down the drawing-room, playing the bagpipe chanter. There is nothing intrinsically wrong with this, yet my recollection is that it created a sense of unease.

This sensation was increased when my mother, going into his room to make the bed, found scented talcum powder on the dressing-table. Those were innocent days. My mother was mildly puzzled by the discovery, but no more. My father, when she told him, took action with uncharacteristic speed. Within hours we were once more tutorless.

There was a brief interval during which we were taught by an ageing ex-schoolmaster, Mr Yoe, who came daily an immense distance, by a combination of buses and trains. He was very down-at-heel and had an invalid wife and was so anxious to keep the job that his hand permanently shook.

During his short term of office Mac came back and was with us again. His effect on Mr Yoe was instantaneous. Whenever Mac came into the room poor Mr Yoe would rise, and stand in respectful silence, as though in the presence of his superior officer, until he went out again. It was somehow faintly cruel and undignified, yet I suppose it was not Mac's fault. It was just that he had that effect on people.

Poor Mr Yoe's term of office was brief. He left when his wife became too ill to be on her own all day. We never heard another word from him – I fear we never enquired. The latter end of the 'shabby-genteel', in those days, must have been appalling; it isn't pleasant at any time. I hope at least we didn't unthinkingly add to his miseries in any way; but I can't be too sure of it.

After two failures my parents must have had some doubts about the wisdom of their plan. As for the rest of the Cornwall Road, what with my father's curious affliction and the continual arrival and departure of horse cabs at the front door, I should think they had already written us off as dangerously nonconformist and financially unreliable. So we were. The appearance of a resident tutor in such a household could only have confirmed their opinion and added to our air of ramshackle grandeur.

No doubt thinking of Cameron, my parents, and particularly my father, were very careful in their next choice, which was the Captain Wilson of the opening chapter, who ran through the house with the warning cry of 'Barouche!

Barouche!' as my father's cab approached from Sutton station in the evening.

He was in every way Cameron's antithesis; in fact one might say that my parents had overcompensated. Extremely popular with all the local ladies, he was a better than average club cricketer and became a regular number two or three batsman for Sutton Wanderers. In appearance he was a shortish, fattish, jovial sort of man whose sense of fun was well in tune with that of his charges, while as a scholar one had the comfortable feeling that he was little more than a half page, so to speak, in front of us.

What endeared him to us as a teacher was that our brief morning lessons were clearly as boring to him as they were to ourselves – especially in summertime. One of his ways of relieving this was by carrying on a running mock-flirtation out of the dining-room window with my Aunt Mabel in the garden next door.

He would pace up and down, the French grammar in his hand, while the sun shone outside and we all three cast imploring glances in the direction of the clock. Pausing at the window he would read: '*Je suis, tu es, il est* . . . or shall we say *elle est*?' then, looking hopefully for some kind of diversion in the next-door garden and seeing Aunt Mabel, who was very short, trying to pick a lilac from a high bush, he would call out, 'Ah! What a beautiful picture! Lilac time!'

My aunt pretending to ignore him, he would try again in his most elaborately gallant manner: 'May I come round and lift you up?'

My brother and I, delighted with this kind of entertainment – or any other form of interruption – would make an appreciative audience while my aunt, who my mother maintained encouraged this sort of thing, tried not to smile.

Aware of his success he would continue the lesson in a voice loud enough to carry over the dividing privet hedge. 'Now then,' he would say, looking next door to mark the effect, 'translate this – *Les tantes les plus grandes ne sont pas toujours les plus belles.'*

In other ways, too, he showed a disarming lack of pedantry. At the end of a quiet session when we had been working out the sums he set us and he had been studying runners and form in the morning paper, my brother told him he'd finished.

'Ah yes,' he said, reluctantly withdrawing his attention from the more absorbing subject of starting prices. 'What do you make the answer?'

'It doesn't go out exactly,' said my brother. 'There's a remainder of 2974.'

Captain Wilson skimmed through the answers at the end of the book. His face fell slightly. It was only five minutes to knocking-off time and the sun was shining.

'That doesn't appear to be the precise answer given in the book. It says here, "Remainder 58".'

This was a setback for all of us.

'Oh dear,' said my brother, then hopefully, 'but my answer is exactly the same as Miss Langley-Smith's telephone number, sir. Two, nine, seven, four. Don't you remember? I heard you ringing her up last night.'

'Dash my buttons, so it is. Well, put a tick against it, my lad. Must be right – and if it isn't it ought to be. Come on, that's enough for this morning. Outside – and one of you bring the golf clubs!'

If we didn't learn a great deal in the academic sense, there was much of lasting value that he could teach us in other ways. His whole attitude to my father was an education in itself. Knowing that my father's chief joy was in getting other people to do jobs in the garden, Captain Wilson would strip off his coat at the first sound of the returning cab and run down the row of spinach that he'd promised to pick, cutting it off with the long-handled shears, while my brother hastily raked up the leaves behind him. Then, quickly putting his hands under the kitchen tap, he would wipe them over his brow. His casual appearance through the garden door a few moments later, mopping his face with a handkerchief, would put my father in a good mood for the whole evening.

On one occasion he must have felt it particularly necessary to be on good terms with my father so, taking advantage of his immobility, he stationed himself, rose catalogue in hand, just behind his deckchair and out of his line of vision while my brother and I watched and listened from the bedroom window above. Catching our eye he put his finger to his lips. Consulting the catalogue he said; 'Caroline Testout is a lovely climber I always think, don't you, sir?'

My father was delighted. None of us had ever before taken the slightest interest in his beloved roses.

'Er, yes. It's one of my favourites,' he answered. 'But as a matter of fact that isn't actually Caroline Testout. That's Mrs Henry Bloggs.'

We watched Captain Wilson stalling as he hastily turned to

the index. 'Bloggs, Mrs Henry.' But he was equal to anything.

'Yes, yes, of course.' Hastily turning pages. 'Caroline Testout blooms much later than this. Besides, it generally prefers an east wall, doesn't it?' Flushed with success, you couldn't stop him. 'By the way you don't believe in much disbudding, I see.'

Upstairs at the back bedroom window we were delighted. Disbudding! That was masterly. Worthy of Aunt Mabel.

'Well I can't get anybody to do it,' my father answered. 'You'd think the boys might take a little interest sometimes; but nobody seems to care a damn about the blessed garden but me.'

This was beginning to sound too much like an appeal for volunteers. Captain Wilson adroitly changed tack. Turning over the page he said, 'You feed a good bone manure, I suppose?' My father was in raptures. Bone manure. Here was a man after his own heart.

'And always give them a good mulching in early spring,' he said, warming to the thought. 'Right back in March or even

February. That's the secret. A chap on the train was saying only the other day, "How in the world is it that old Connie's got a rose in his buttonhole all the year round? How does he do it . . . ?"'

Later that night, as they were going to bed, he said to my mother, 'You know that fellow Wilson's quite a decent sort of chap. I think he ought to be very good for those two boys, don't you, Norah?'

'Do you, Steph dear?' my mother answered. 'Try not to put your hands on the top of the dressing-table, if you don't mind. Lizzie's just polished it.'

After he had been with us about a month my mother paid one of her rare visits to London. Though Sutton was such a short distance away – in fact a suburb – she went up very seldom and my brother and I hardly at all. A trip to London was just as much of an event for us as it would be now for somebody living in, say, the north of Scotland. The barrier was more mental than physical. You were either a 'London-going type' or you were not. Aunt Mabel was. The place clearly drew her and she was much criticised for it, even in our household. We thought these trips to the theatre, or whatever it might be, a sign of dangerous instability. My mother only went when the need for pillowcases or table napkins made a visit to Gorringe's unavoidable – never just for pleasure.

So we were left on our own for the day with Captain Wilson. We were not particularly surprised when, towards the end of the morning, he set us some work and announced that he was going down to Sutton High Street to buy a paper. We already knew the importance in life of the midday racing edition and felt much sympathy for him in his need.

We finished the work he set us – or at least did as much of it as we judged could pass without too much loss of self-respect, and waited. Lunchtime came and still no Captain Wilson. Lizzie appeared at the door, blank-faced and uncomplaining, to know whether we would like to start without him. Eventually he appeared, cycling up the Cornwall Road on one of the bicycles of unknown origin that families tend to accumulate. He came in, beaming in all directions, and took off his cycle clips. He seemed unaware of being late for lunch or that Lizzie was hovering, expressionless, in the background. He was clearly delighted to see us again.

'We've done all the work you set us, sir, ages ago,' my brother said. 'Would you like to correct the maths?'

He seemed faintly surprised. 'What about the Latin?'

'You didn't set us any Latin, sir. Just some French to learn and the maths.'

'Oh, didn't I?' He took the exercise book my brother held out to him and examined it closely. 'What's this then?'

'That's not Latin, sir, that's maths. That you set us before you went out.'

He seemed puzzled by the whole situation. 'Maths?'

'Yes sir – sums,' I said, hoping to make things clearer.

'Oh maths.' He understood at once.

'That you gave us to do, sir,' my brother continued. 'Would you like to correct it now? Only I think Lizzie wants to lay the table.'

He didn't seem to hear. 'Right,' he said, 'well let's have a look, then. Let's see what you've been up to.'

My brother put the exercise book on the dining-room table. Lizzie gave up and went back into the kitchen.

Captain Wilson looked at the book a moment, then turned suspiciously to my brother. 'This isn't Latin,' he said.

'No sir, maths.'

'That you set us, sir,' I explained, 'before you went out.'

'Oh, maths! Yes – of course.'

We got through lunch somehow. Captain Wilson was ami-ability itself, but it was only when he missed the edge of the table with his glass for the second time that the full implication finally became clear to us. We were actually in the presence of Drunkenness. This was something that of course we'd read about in newspapers, heard jokes about or come across in books – but here it was in our own dining-room. We were two boys, alone in a house with a Drunken Man – except of course for Lizzie, but she didn't count. We were thrilled. This was Life – Drama – the most exciting thing that had happened to our family since my father's cab horse had bolted.

We could hardly wait for the return of my mother. The afternoon seemed endless. Captain Wilson had gone upstairs for a 'little nap' and had not reappeared. When at last we saw my mother come in the front gate, we besieged her, positively dancing round her as she walked up the front garden path. 'He was drunk, Mum, honestly he was,' we said, excitedly. We had slight scruples about letting him down in this way, but the sheer grandeur of the news swept everything aside.

'Tiddley,' we added. 'Blotto,' we explained, hanging on to her arm and peering up into her face. They were the only words we knew.

'He kept knocking things off the table.'

'And when I tried to show him my maths book he didn't know what it was.'

'He thought it was Latin!' We both burst out laughing from sheer elation.

My mother was not amused. Once again, when my father came home, there was a conclave behind closed doors, while we waited, unable to settle to a serious game, at the bottom of the garden.

Captain Wilson left next morning. Pale and movingly sober he packed up his things and just disappeared.

For a short time several of the local ladies went about as though, in spirit, they wore black armbands, though their husbands' step was correspondingly springy.

In a few weeks he was back again. I don't know how it happened; whether or not my mother was swayed by his rather too obvious charm. I think not. I should say it was much more likely that my father was the one who was prepared to give him a second chance. After all he was admitted by everyone to be a stylish bat, if not a big run-getter, and his sins were those of a 'good chap'.

Before long we were back once more, with our books on the dining-room table, all three of us glancing frequently at the clock and ready for any diversion. The sight of my aunt's figure over the hedge in the next garden would be welcomed by all of us and would bring Captain Wilson to the window in an ecstasy of mock rapture.

'What a charming picture!' he would say, loudly enough for her to hear. '*Les tantes les plus petites sont toujours les plus belles.*' And my aunt, pretending offence, would make a face at him and go indoors.

Everything was just as before. We didn't mind. In fact we were very pleased. We liked him; because in most ways he was really just one of us.

Chapter XVI
My Father's Enlarging Camera

During one of our periods of more than usually acute financial depression my father decided to sell the drawing-room sofa. It had been a wedding present and, typically, was intended for a house much larger than Melton. Nobody sat on it if they could help it because the springs were broken at one end and sagged obscenely below, like the entrails of a gored horse. Besides, its presence in the drawing-room was becoming an increasing nuisance now that the ping-pong table was almost always up. So my father decided to get rid of it. A 'little man' was sent for, to come and value it, with a view to purchase. He came; he saw; he valued. When, eventually, his offer came by letter my father, unsuspecting, opened it at the breakfast table. (He must have been down before we'd finished for once.) The result was dramatic – but then with my father everything was. He flung up his arms and gave a loud cry, as though pierced to the heart.

'Daylight robbery!' he roared. It was one of his favourite phrases. Every bill that he received was greeted in the same way; but in this case the roar was louder – more impressive.

'Be careful of your cup, Steph dear,' my mother said.

'I'd rather take it outside in the road and chop it up,' he shouted, glaring round the table to see if there was any dissent. There wasn't. My brother and I were too busy trying to imagine him in the middle of the Cornwall Road, attacking the drawing-room sofa with a chopper.

The only result was that the sofa was from that day moved out of his sight into the tiny room by the front door, still known as the nursery. It already contained, as well as cupboards full of our own outgrown and broken toys, several bags of my father's old golf clubs, the ping-pong table when not in use, and anything else that was too dilapidated to remain visible.

Once broken, nothing in our household was ever mended. It was not until many years later that it ever occurred to me that this was not necessarily so in other people's homes. The system in our house was that anything that was likely to bring my father face to face with the reality of our situation was to be stowed away out of sight. He never came into the nursery, so by the end of our time at Melton you couldn't get into the room at all, except by jumping on to the back of the drawing-room sofa and stepping from there on to the top of the other various derelict bits of furniture that had come to rest there.

My father, too, was a great collector of pictures, which he seemed to have acquired as payment for bad debts. In a way he was surprisingly modest, because I don't remember that he ever had one of his own painstaking but rather charming sketches framed. They were much better than the dreary imitations of Birket Foster in their awful gilt frames, or the sweet Victorian maidens coyly peeping from beneath umbrellas that plastered almost every inch of our drawing-room walls.

Not quite every inch though, as I remember; because once, using my fountain pen as a machine gun and firing from the hip with the filling lever cocked, I turned in a rapid half circle with the intention of 'shooting' my brother and sprayed the faded shot-silk-and-roses wallpaper liberally with a stream of ink which stayed there for as long as we remained in the house.

One of my father's favourite pictures, a large, smoke-blackened oil of a mountain scene in a very heavy gilt frame that hung over the stairs, one day fell with an enormous crash and bounced down into the hall, luckily without killing anybody. It remained, face inwards, against the nursery wall from that day onward; but the torn piece of wallpaper that it brought down with it remained permanently hanging above the stairs.

Nobody attempted to stick it back up again, or even to tear it off. A kind of defeatism had settled over the whole household by this time. What had started off with such high hopes in the house that my father designed for his bride on their marriage was disintegrating visibly every day. The furniture he's bought then, or designed himself, was far too big and ornate for Melton. One by one the pieces suffered the same fate as the drawing-room sofa.

The one exception was the dining-room table. It was made of heavy, fumed oak, oval at the ends, and matched the very solid dining chairs with their brass-studded, red-leather seats and headrests. My father had designed it and had it specially made in the first mad financial flush of his marriage. The two end chairs, on which my mother and father sat, had arms, one of which was already broken when I can first remember it. Mac later completed the job by sitting on the oval, unsupported end of the table and breaking it too. It didn't break right off, but cracked down at a slight angle.

Contrary to the accepted customs of the house he tried to mend it. He turned it upside down, I remember, and tried to hammer a rough piece of board across the crack, as a support; but the nails he used were slightly too long and appeared through the polished surface of the top, while the partly broken flap still hung down exactly as before. My father's system of complete *laissez-faire* was really better.

Our nursery, then, had become a symbol for the whole family state of mind, a receptacle for facts too painful to be faced – a kind of collective family subconscious. But there were some things too large and too impossible even for the nursery. In this category I suppose one might place my mother's cello. She had tried to learn, briefly, as a girl, but without success, and the residual instrument, now without a back, remained in its case, leaning against the drawing-room wall, all the time we lived at Melton. It was rather a nuisance when, towards the end, the room was completely given up to cards and table-tennis, but one just had to accept it as one of the natural hazards.

But the thing which, to me, symbolizes our whole family life most completely was my father's enlarging camera. He had bought it in the early days of their marriage. I don't know why. Neither did my mother. He was not a particularly keen photographer, yet something or someone had at some moment of his life persuaded him that it was what he wanted; so he bought it.

This had all happened at a period too far back in time for me to remember. All I knew was that in the cycle shed there was a large wooden crate against which I rested my bicycle. I had done this without thought for many years when some whim prompted me to ask my mother what was in it.

'Your father's enlarging camera,' she said in the neutral voice that she used on such occasions.

This in no way struck me as odd; nor did the fact that it had never yet been opened. It was not the sort of thing that did seem odd in our family.

Chapter XVII
Family Games

If I have given the impression that ours was an unhappy household, oppressed by an increasing degree of genteel poverty, this was far from the case – at least until latterly. The presence of Mac could certainly be oppressive, when he set out to make it so; but this was not always. Sport of all kinds was the family obsession. My father was at his best and happiest when recalling his own exploits in the days before his mysterious affliction struck him down. Just as he was a mental gardener he was also a mental golfer and would sit in the back garden for hours on a summer evening, sucking the ring on the end of his pencil and playing his way round Banstead Downs or his holy of holies, Walton Heath. Cluttering up our nursery were the golf clubs of his mobile days; strange, hickory-shafted things with such splendidly nostalgic names as 'baffy', 'cleek', 'niblick', or 'lofting iron'. No semi-anonymous, steel-shafted implements dignified only by numbers.

As our household became more and more male-dominated with the advent of Mac, so the obsession with sport increased. I can remember the state of excitement with which we waited, in those pre-radio days, for the arrival of the paper on the morning after Joe Beckett had fought Georges Carpentier. Later, when the elegant and glamorous Frenchman challenged the great Jack Dempsey for the Heavyweight Championship of the World, a newspaper chartered an aircraft to fly over south London showing the result by coloured lights – green for Carpentier and red for Dempsey.

I can remember the groan of dismay at Melton as we heard the plane, then saw the red light come on.

In 1921 we suffered greatly as a household when Warwick Armstrong's Australians, with Gregory and McDonald, their great pair of fast bowlers, were decimating an MCC eleven which included even the legendary Jack Hobbs.

Nobody, as I remember, spoke about matters of national importance. Indeed, by the standards of Melton these sporting events were the matters of national importance. Such things as the Locarno Pact and the Zinoviev Letter, if they were ever mentioned, left no impression whatever in my mind.

Towards the end of the Melton period, when table tennis was permanently installed in the drawing-room, to the exclusion of almost everything else, and the rhythmic sound of bat and ball were practically continuous, one couldn't help feeling that this frenzy of noisy activity was really some largely unconscious cover-up for the seething divisions and discontents that must have been working away below the surface.

For those not engaged in table tennis there was still just enough room up by the fireplace for the card table. There was also a game called Puff Billiards, played on a special, circular board, in which the players each had a thing like an old-fashioned motor horn, fixed on a swivelled mounting, which one squeezed furiously, with various degrees of success, in an attempt to blow a cork ball into one's opponent's pocket while keeping it out of one's own.

Better still was a game called Wibbly-Wob, which almost defies description. Briefly, a small object like a miniature ice-hockey puck had to be propelled across the table – our dining-room table – and into one's opponent's goal by means of a small, wedge-shaped piece of wood attached by a long, flexible piece of wire to a handle which one held, prodding madly at the 'wob' while the head of one's 'wibbler' swung in all directions and was almost impossible to control.

The sense of frustration and impotence with which one attempted to prod the moving object was something which quickly reduced everyone to a state of hysteria and, in some cases, violence. It was during a game of Wibbly-Wob that Mac, unable to defend his goal by normal means, sat on the table and broke off the end.

No game was too juvenile. For a time my father and Mac, taking their cue from my brother and myself, became obsessed by conkers. My father would come back from London with his pockets mysteriously bulging while Mac brought his back from Paris. For a time even cards had to take a second place and the evenings rang with the sound of conker striking conker, then the particular sound of a shattered conker bouncing off bits of drawing-room furniture followed by shouts of triumph and accusations of unfair play.

During this craze my father, for some reason, was given a box at one of the London theatres. No doubt it was in pay-ment of a bad debt from a dubious business associate, but it was something so rare for any member of our family that it was not to be refused. It came at a particularly crucial moment in the conker season. My mother, naturally, was keen to go.

She never went anywhere, while they, at least, got out of the house during the day, etcetera, etcetera. In the end there was a compromise; they went, but during the interval produced their conkers and sat there – in the white tie and tails of the period – playing until the curtain went up again.

But it was while Captain Wilson was with us that the sport mania reached its zenith. He could hardly have come to a better house. Not content with the usual games, he invented his own. A particular favourite was Hoicky Hockey, played on the tennis lawn with a football and walking sticks. This, as I remember it, was strictly what would now be called a 'contact sport' – the chief contact being the highly nubile eighteen-year-old daughter of the local parson, who had taken to appearing as soon as our morning lessons were finished – or perhaps it would be more correct to say that our lessons had taken to finishing as soon as she appeared.

My brother and I found her sudden interest in our household both inexplicable and rather to be deplored, while her all too apparent femininity struck a new and ominous note.

It was under the guidance of Captain Wilson that we turned the whole garden, and some of the field behind, into a nine-hole, approach-and-putt golf course. Naturally, the space was a bit restricted, but with a little ingenuity we got by. There was one interesting hole where one had to play a full mashie shot from the field at the back, over the fence and on to the tennis court, with enough back-spin to stop it going into the flowerbeds or the rockery. Anything slightly over-pitched would have landed on the crazy-paving terrace and bounced up, almost certainly, through the drawing-room window.

Curiously enough I can't ever remember this happening.

Another intriguing, dog-leg hole was one in which the tee was in the front garden and one had to play a carefully controlled shot, just missing the corner of the house, and pitching somewhere in the vegetable garden. From here an 'explosive' bunker-type shot could bring you over the yard and into the back garden again. A badly played tee shot might leave one with a very difficult lie, and picking out was against the rules.

The most dreaded hazard, though, was the concrete yard at the side of the house. This had to be carried with one's tee shot and failure to do so brought very serious trouble. It was small and completely enclosed, with a high wooden gate at each end. Not only was the playing surface concrete, but it was slightly sloped, so that one's ball always ran down to the bottom gate. The local rule was that this gate could not be opened, so the only possible way to get out of an otherwise permanent trap was to batter one's ball egg-shaped till it would go underneath. My brother once took fifty-seven strokes to play this one hole, spoiling an otherwise excellent round.

Chapter XVIII
The Great Stefanini Hoax

Mac was not with us when Captain Wilson joined the household. He was at Melton only intermittently, as the circumstances of his strange and adventurous life permitted. His jobs abroad brought, to me at least, a great lifting of the spirit, though I would never have dared to admit it, even in the safety of my own mind. There was one particularly long and oppressive summer when he had a job writing the words 'Daily Mail' in exhaust smoke over such places as Epsom Downs on Derby Day – 'sky writing' as it was called. Mercifully it is an art-form which seems to have died out; possibly because, by the time the aircraft had reached the final 'l' of 'Mail' most of the 'Daily' had disintegrated. Besides, as Mac himself admitted, he found it difficult enough to spell on the ground, let alone in the air.

Even when he was away for some months the little single bedroom at the top of the stairs remained unmistakably his – full of his own possessions and, in his absence, exuding a powerful distillation of his personality.

It was strange how Mac had the power to dominate our house, even from the other side of the world. He had to a marked extent the male attribute of staking out his territory and guarding it against other males. Melton was his. Anyone else setting foot in it would have to reckon with him.

One wonders now, unavoidably, at all the implications of

this. How, for instance, did my father fit in? He was, so to speak, the 'sitting male', in more senses than one. Mac's jealous dominance of the house would seem to suggest that he had surrendered his position in some way. My recollection, filtered through many years of memory, tells me that this was not so. It seems to me that both Mac and my father looked upon our house chiefly as some sort of club, where one could meet in the evening for a game of cards and a discussion on the day's play in the Test Match, and where meals of a sort were eventually served.

If that is so then where did my mother come into it? Or did she come into it at all? That is a question which the succeeding years have not answered.

After the arrival and final acceptance of Captain Wilson, then, Mac's next return home from abroad was awaited with some anxiety – though not, one felt, by Captain Wilson himself. By the time Mac arrived he was already well in, especially where my father was concerned. Though he was no card player he was far more knowledgeable on the subject of first-class batting averages than Mac, who was, surprisingly, no sportsman.

From the first it was a clash of wills. As human beings the two protagonists could hardly have been more different; Captain Wilson florid, urbane, pipe-smoking, clubbable – Mac dark, saturnine, handsome, ominous.

On his first evening home Mac pinned my mother with his notorious pale glare.

'What the hell's that fellow doing here, Norah?' he said as soon as Captain Wilson had gone out of the room. She told him. He merely gave an incredulous snort of disgust and left it at that for the moment.

A few days later he was about to mount the Norton at the front gate when he looked up and saw Captain Wilson in his room. *His* room – Mac's sacred territory.

'Found what you want, old chap?' he called up, in his most offensive manner.

'Yes thank you,' Captain Wilson answered, smiling pleasantly.

Mac had met his match at last. But he needn't have worried; the seeds of his own destruction lay within Captain Wilson's easy-going, cheerful soul. They needed no cultivation by anybody else.

Other jobs took Mac away and the tensions slackened again, at least for a time. It was at this moment that Pix next door sprang upon us the news that she, too, was about to take in a lodger, a Frenchman, known to a friend of hers, who wanted to spend the summer months with an English family. Whether this was an attempt by Belhaven to outbid Melton in the matter of bizarre lodgers or merely a financial convenience I don't know.

A Frenchman – in the Cornwall Road! The whole thing seems so improbable in retrospect that one can hardly believe it.

But if it seems improbable now it seemed no less so to us then. This time Pix had really excelled herself. Captain Stefanini's arrival was awaited with a joyful curiosity in Melton – and by none more than Captain Wilson. To him it seemed a fine opportunity to exploit the situation with a little harmless fun at my aunt's expense; and, as usual, we were his willing accomplices.

The plan was quite simple. Captain Stefanini was due to arrive by train that evening, when Uncle Ath would be at home to meet him. Captain Wilson's harmless, indeed almost pointless, joke was to ring Belhaven much earlier in the person of the unknown Frenchman, to announce his imminent arrival, plus a fictitious manservant and dog, while my aunt was in the house alone. Having thrown her into a state of suitable alarm and confusion he would go round next door and confess that it was all just a bit of neighbourly fun.

That was the idea; but unfortunately practical jokes nearly always misfire. This one didn't just misfire, it backfired. We could hardly wait to finish our lessons that morning. Neither could Captain Wilson. The clock on the dining-room mantelpiece was still well short of the hour when he beamed happily upon us and said, 'Well, that'll do for this morning, I think.'

Glowing with anticipation we put our books away and prepared ourselves to take part in this splendid Practical Joke or Jape, as the heroes of the school stories and comics of the time would have called it. To us the most exquisite part of the whole thing was that, by stationing ourselves in the bay window and standing – in our outdoor shoes most probably – on the red leather seats of the dining-room chairs we could see, above the intervening privet hedge, my aunt in the corresponding bay window next door, answering Captain Wilson's call – not ten feet away.

This seemed to us the quintessence of ironic humour.

Captain Wilson, winking at us to keep silent, picked up the

phone and asked for the number, quite normally.

'Sutton one O nine two, please.'

We held our breath. Faintly through two panes of glass and a privet hedge we heard the next-door phone ring. A moment later we saw my aunt, a keen telephonist, come in and lift the receiver.

Captain Wilson, a yard away but safely out of view of the window, began by saying 'Ullo? Ullo?' in what he hoped sounded like a French accent.

We saw a look of slight doubt come over my aunt's face.

'Is zat Madame – how-you-say-Constan-dooros?'

It was a thoroughly ham performance. One felt it could hardly have deceived a child; but if it didn't deceive us it delighted us. We stuffed our hands into our mouths in our silent joy.

'Here is Stefanini,' Captain Wilson, said, beginning to warm up. 'Stefanini from Paris.'

Through the hedge we could faintly see, but not hear, my aunt's reaction.

'I'm already here, at the Gare du Londres, Victoria, with my man and my leetle dawg.'

We saw the look of horror on my aunt's face. It was working better than anybody could have dared to hope. We rolled about, hugging ourselves.

'Yes, yes,' repeated Captain Wilson, piling it on, 'Wiz my, 'ow you say, servant-man and my leetle dawg.' He obviously enjoyed saying 'leetle dawg'.

'I come at once. Quickly,' he said, winking again in our direction.

That is where he should have stopped; but like many practical jokers, he lacked the sensitivity to recognize the moment. Instead of disclosing himself and enjoying his small and rather infantile triumph at my aunt's expense he continued to the end. In the other house we saw my aunt put back the receiver with a look of stunned disbelief.

We jumped off our chairs and offered our congratulations. They were absolutely sincere; we were full of admiration.

'You should have seen her face,' we said.

'Honestly, I wish you could have seen her,' we gasped, rolling about with pleasure.

Together we waited for the sound of the gate and the rat-tat at the front door, which was the usual reaction from either sister when faced with a domestic emergency. None came. We climbed back on to the dining-room chairs and looked next door. She was on the telephone to somebody, gesticulating with her free hand and clearly under some emotional stress.

This was not the anticipated reaction. Something had gone wrong. It always does on these occasions. Before long my aunt did come round. We heard her voice in the kitchen, talking to my mother. It was the voice of one who is not amused. Silently we crept out of the drawing-room door into the garden – all three of us – and played golf 'out at the back', a safe distance from the house.

We learned later what had happened. My aunt, completely taken in by Captain Wilson's performance, had not unnaturally rung up my uncle at his office in London and he had gone at once to Victoria Station, where he spent a fruitless morning accosting anybody with a dog.

It was too late to apologize. In any case apologies at that moment were not acceptable. In the meantime the real Captain Stefanini rang to say that he had arrived, unaccompanied, at Cheam station, not Sutton as expected, and what should he do? There were no cabs at Cheam station; in fact there was no transport of any kind; so Captain Wilson, in an attempt at expiation, was obliged to go there as fast as possible on foot and help carry the visitor's bags for him. It was quite a long way from Cheam station to the Cornwall Road. What they talked about and how Captain Wilson, with his limited French, explained the situation I can't imagine.

Eventually, though, relations between Melton and Belhaven were restored to their old footing – at least as far as my aunt was concerned. Uncle Ath, I feel, never quite recovered and continued to look at Captain Wilson, when obliged to, coldly and in silence, with head tilted back, below his glasses.

But it was not the Stefanini incident that brought Captain Wilson's time in our household to an end, nor was it in any way the work of Mac; though I'm sure he would have hastened it if he had been there to do so. Eventual disaster was inevitable. It caught up with him at the local cricket club dance where he became spectacularly drunk and fell heavily in the middle of the dance floor, bringing down several local reputations with him. This time there was no reprieve. He left the next morning, with some of the funds from the night before. During the next few weeks we had to answer many enquiries for his address from angry tradesmen and slightly embarrassed local ladies.

Chapter XIX
Forgotten Heroes

There is a particular time of year that most clearly brings back the essence of those early suburban days. It is June, and for preference it would be soon after breakfast. For some reason which hardly needs specifying, my brother and I have not gone to school. We are sitting out on the concrete steps that lead down from the drawing-room door to the crazy paving and rockery mentally designed by my father, filling in yesterday's Wimbledon results from the morning paper in the official programme which, somehow, we always managed to acquire as early as possible in the meeting.

This was a ritual labour of love which had to be pursued to the last set of the most inconspicuous first-round mixed double. Outside the heat is already bouncing up from the asphalt pavements to mingle with the scent of privet and laburnum – the essential smell of suburbia and my childhood, just as the noise of ball on racquet, the crying of the score in next-door gardens, is its essential sound – and my eyes are beginning to prick with the first intimations of hay fever.

Wimbledon, the taste of strawberries, and hay fever; they are all lumped together, for good or ill, in my mind. Though for my brother and myself, sitting on the back steps in our floppy grey felt hats, strawberries and cream were modified into the speciality of the house, a 'Banana and Swiss' – the

Swiss, of course, being Nestlé's Swiss Milk. It was to us almost what a whisky and soda was to my father; a built-in part of everyday life. Best of all when one was asked to scrape out the tin. Scrape one did, both the sides and the bottom, first one way, then crossways, to make sure that absolutely nothing was left, and finally the semi-crystallized bits round the jagged rim left by the tin opener. I can taste it in retrospect now, as I write.

How I wish I still had one of those Wimbledon programmes of the period. I know that to glance down the list of players would reveal long forgotten names that would magically recreate the moment. Everyone knows the names Tilden, Borotra, Miss Ryan and Mlle Lenglen – they are part of sporting history – but who remembers Mavrogordato, Donisthorpe, H. Roper Barrett and Mrs Satterthwaite? Yet every time I dredge one of these up from the remote past it comes like a nugget of gold. And those splendid initials – B. I. C Norton, A. R. F. Kingscote, O. G. N. Turnbull, G. R. O. Crole-Rees – they still sound like an incantation or a fanfare. Does anyone have initials like that now? Of course they don't.

Nor was it only tennis players. There was P. G. H. Fender, the wily Surrey cricket captain, C. J. H. Tolley, mighty hitter of a golf ball and, surpassing them all, the captain of Essex and, if I remember, the MCC itself, J. W. H. T. ('Jonny-Won't-Hit-Today') Douglas. These, and alas many others who have completely faded from my mind, were the heroes of my childhood, and the man who brought them alive for me and who remains perhaps the greatest – and least honoured – hero of them all was Tom Webster, for many years the sporting cartoonist of the *Daily Mail*.

I wonder how many people still remember him? In my opinion he was a minor genius, still imitated, though to me never equalled, by generations of cartoonists who by now probably don't even know his name. Yet among older race-goers there must be some who remember 'Tishy', the racehorse with corkscrew front legs, or Fender's sweater, or the tennis player who threw the ball up so high when he served that he would sit beside the court and wait for a messenger boy to appear and warn him when it was coming down.

As far as I know he was the innovator of the cartoon in which drawings and letterpress mingled to tell a story, often some tiny incident that only he had noticed, such as the moth that darted in and out of the lights over the billiard table on which two champions were playing, which he built up into something more interesting than the game itself. His style was absolutely free. Both letterpress and drawings appeared to come straight from the pen, uncorrected, with a vitality that a more careful method would have killed. Some of his likenesses were brilliant, though inevitably some people escaped him. He was not especially successful with women, I seem to remember; though, of course, in those unenlightened days they were hardly part of the sporting scene. But his real genius lay in the pinpointing of some small, often unconscious idiosyncrasy of behaviour or movement – the particular set of the shoulders as a bowler walked back to begin his run after having an LBW appeal refused – that suddenly, in a few strokes, encapsulated a particular man in a way that one recognized as a true flash of insight if, later, one saw the man himself.

I know nothing at all of Tom Webster's life beyond once

reading that he was completely untaught. I can quite believe it. His gift was an acute spontaneity and an observation that would have been ruined by a self-conscious technique.

I make no apologies for this digression to do honour to one who played such a part in the formative years of my childhood. Each year he brought out a collection of his best cartoons, in a paper cover – costing, I suppose, about half-a-crown – and each year I bought it. I wish I had them now. To turn over those pages would bring back the sound of my brother's collection of dance records – '78s of course, played with a steel needle – and heroes of another kind: Paul Whiteman and his band ('Whispering', with swannee whistle accompaniment), Zez Confrey ('Kitten on the Keys') and, in after years, Layton and Johnson and 'The Two Black Crows'.

But we are still on the back steps, filling in our programmes. My father's cab has clattered away and the summer day is before us. What shall we do? Go out somewhere on our bikes? Play some secret, childish game with lead soldiers, as we used to in the happy, unsophisticated days before the advent of Mac? We don't know – we don't greatly care. It would be a long time before the returning adults would disturb our peace. Time's wingèd chariot is completely inaudible on a June morning when one is only twelve years old. The nearest we got to it was the familiar sound of the 'one o'clock shunter' some distance away up at Sutton station, the clash of buffer on buffer, in a ripple effect, down a line of trucks, reduced by the distance to a mere part of the background and significant of nothing more urgent than that Lizzie would soon be appearing outside the back door in her faded blue apron to call out that dinner was ready.

Chapter XX
On Going to Bed

This feeling of limitless security, though, was confined to the summer mornings. It is a truism to say that each day is a microcosm of life itself, even for a twelve-year-old. By tea-time, even on the best of summer days, doubts are beginning to creep into the periphery of the mind. Games which, immediately after breakfast, held such promise are becoming tedious and one wishes one hadn't brought quite so many things out of the house, all of which must be put back again out of sight before the ominous sound of my father's cab brings an end to one's sense of freedom.

If each new morning was, in those days, a rebirth then it is as well, for the sake of honesty, to remember that each evening was also in its way a little death. Intimations of mortality would begin with the fading light. Somewhere beyond Cheam, in Nonsuch Park so my father said, there were a pair of peacocks whose eerily romantic cry at nightfall, like lost spirits, seemed oddly out of place in the ordinariness of the Cornwall Road. Yet with the onset of dusk even Melton became less than ordinary and, in winter when the curtains were drawn, even a little sinister.

This I would know in my heart, though of course I would never admit it to anyone.

Sometimes as we played our last game before my mother

called us to bed, and while my father sat in the gathering dusk sucking his pencil, there would be a gradually increasing sound in the evening sky – the sound of innumerable wings as vast flocks of starlings flew over, going always from east to west. Occasionally they'd pause for a brief rest on the elm trees of Tabor's Lane that flanked the playing-field of Cheam School. For a few moments the trees would be alive with a babel of throats and then, as if by some telepathic signal, they'd instantaneously take to the air again and leave the tree silent, but white with droppings.

This was such a regular part of the summer evening that no one, to my knowledge, ever questioned it or tried to find out the answer to the simple question – where were they going? And if they were returning every evening from London, as they clearly were, how did they get up there in the first place – and why?

No doubt somebody more knowledgeable could give the simple explanation. Most probably they passed over in the mornings, going the other way, while we were asleep, so that we never saw them. But why should thousands of starlings live in the outer suburbs and commute to London every day? This at once poses a number of interesting ornithological and even sociological questions, but I'm afraid I don't know the answers.

The passing overhead of the starlings was the moment at which the thoughtless certainties of the day began to melt into the irrational fears of night-time. I knew that the time was soon coming when, being the youngest of the household, I should have to say goodnight to those cheerful, well-lit, well-filled rooms downstairs and go alone into that other world upstairs; a world of dark landings and drawn curtains where anything might lie in wait. One would think that a small, over-filled suburban villa could hold no terrors; but for a twelve-year-old child it can.

Each night the ordeal would be repeated. I would go the rounds of the table-tennis and card players, pausing at the door for a last look upon sanity and security, while my mother would say: 'Run along then, dear, I'll be up in a moment.'

I knew that she wouldn't – or at least her idea of 'a moment' was not mine.

From the card table my father, intent on his hand, would call out, 'Close the door, would you, boy? There's a howling draught over here.'

There was nothing for it. The moment had come. Not daring to look to either side I would stumble upstairs into that waiting limbo where no one thought to follow me. At the top of the stairs I would run from one light switch to the next, my heart pounding. Inside the bedroom, breathless, I would switch on the glaring central light and stare round. Nothing. But that didn't in the least reassure me. There were still dark places under the bed and behind the door where It could hide; but to find out I would have to move away from the wall and expose my back.

This feeling that something evil and unseen would get behind me was the worst of all. For years I undressed with my back pressed to the bedroom wall, in secret terror, while gusts of normal noise and laughter came from the crowded, well-lit world below. Eventually I would hear the door downstairs open and the voices become louder. My brother saying good-night and the others answering him. Blessed, blessed sound! Immediately the tension would drop away and, inwardly shamefaced, I'd move out from the wall before my brother came in.

Dreadful though these evenings genuinely were, I do not think I ever so much as contemplated the even more dreadful alternative of admitting my fear. It now seems hard to im-agine why. I suppose the simple reason was that my fear of the Ancient Mariner's frightful fiend was not as great as the fear of being laughed at. I don't think, though, that my parents would have laughed. I'm quite sure my mother wouldn't, and my father, though he might not have been particularly con-cerned or understanding, would certainly not have laughed. That sort of unkindness was not in him. But Mac would. Or he wouldn't actually have laughed; he would have pinned me with his cold, unsmiling eyes and said: 'Norah dear, your little boysy wants you to put him to beddy-byes' – and the blow to one's private self-esteem would have been worse and more lasting than the possibility of any frightful fiend.

But with the appearance of my brother all was changed. We shared the small back bedroom and, once my mother had been in to say a final 'goodnight', we would allow ourselves to be taken over by a private fantasy world which must have been lurking somewhere in the subconscious and which I now recall imperfectly and with some embarrassment.

In our nursery days I had owned a stuffed animal vaguely resembling a white cat, known as 'Beggerman'. Around this battered creature – which in spite of its name was declared to be female – there rose a whole elaborate mythology which was released only when the bedroom light was out, in a series of spontaneously improvised stories known under the general title of 'Beggerman Tales'. The whole private ceremony of tale-telling was hedged about with a kind of secret ritual – the sort of ritual that children love to create and which probably goes back to some long-forgotten tribal instinct.

First my brother, using a particular form of words, would ask to be told a tale. This I would as formally refuse to do, using a set response. My brother would then counter this with a further request, differently but correctly phrased, which I would again refuse while frantically searching in my mind for subject matter; because I knew that, once a few precious moments had been gained, the rules of the game demanded that I should give in.

Once having succumbed to this pressure, my mind whirling in an apparent vacuum, my practice was generally to begin, slowly and dramatically, with the words, 'Bang! Bang! Bang!' and, during the time it took to say them, pray that some inspiration would come to me out of the darkness. As an opening, it is not ideally easy to follow, and the thought of having to do so instantaneously, without premeditation, now appals me.

Very little has remained to me of that private world and what there is one views with a kind of horrified disbelief for what it reveals.

Part human, part cat, Beggerman was queen of an imaginary country which, of course, to some extent mirrored the wartime world of the Cornwall Road, yet a Cornwall Road distorted by the largely unconscious thought process of a twelve-year-old; because it was part of the ritual that whenever possible, the words should come before the thoughts, from a sort of limbo between true waking and sleeping.

My brother, I remember, when his turn came, was particularly good at this, because his subconscious could actually produce instant verse, which would pour from his mouth, in the darkness, like Stock Exchange prices from a tape machine; a talent which even then left him by daylight and which was one of those fleeting gifts that seem to die with childhood.

But more of that later.

My brother and I, then, can fairly claim to have invented the 'stream-of-consciousness' method, in the back bedroom at Melton, some years before others, more distinguished, took it over.

As I say, only a few broken fragments of this world still remain; the surviving relics of a whole imaginary civilization. In the realm of which Beggerman was queen there was a shadowy band, a kind of Greek chorus, of roving characters, the Shop Girls (I suppose female shop assistants were a novelty) whose war cry of 'Alcohol! Alcohol!' heard approaching in the distance, struck fear into all. There was also a character called Madcap Maurice, the Mighty Milkman, who careered through the streets in a two-wheel milk float – so like a Roman chariot; easy to see the connection here – and there was also the occasion when Beggerman met the Goddess Venus in a margarine queue.

Most significant though, was Beggerman's faithful servant Annalathora, surely the mirror-image of Lizzie, who was treated by her employer with such anxious consideration that she was never allowed to get up, and remained in bed all day while her mistress did all the work and brought her meals up to her room on a tray.

Though Beggerman and her subjects belonged exclusively to me, they were not the whole of that private fantasy world. To make it even more exclusive we decided on a secret sign – my father was, or had been, a Mason. It was agreed, in the back bedroom at Melton, that, for the rest of our lives, we should shoot out our right fist whenever we used the word 'vivid'.

Even now as I write it, I can hardly prevent a slight movement of the right arm.

As a secret sign it could hardly have been bettered. After all, it isn't the kind of word it is hard to do without. Neither of us ever used it anyway.

Occasionally my powers of invention would fail me completely. I would stick to my first, ritual refusal to tell a Beggerman Tale and mean it. Then it was my turn to pester my brother for a session of instant verse. Like my stories, very little has remained to be handed down to posterity. There was one, though, which I can still remember to have had a fine, ringing opening:

> The thunder raged
> And the sun it shone,
> And everybody was in but John.
> He was up in the belfry tower
> Messing about with some bags of flour.

Then there was a stirring poem in ballad form which began:

> 'Not for ten pounds a minute,'
> Said the mouse with eyes of flame.
> 'Not for ten pounds a minute
> Would I betray his name.
> His head shall blacken on the
> Pikes of all his glories' fame.'

And there, or at some point soon after, sleep would overtake one or both of us.

So far as I know my brother has entirely given up the practice of instant verse. How sad that the unconscious gifts of childhood should always die so soon.

Chapter XXI
Faster! Faster!

With the departure of Captain Wilson, Mac once again had the field completely to himself – which, of course, was the way he liked it. All the more unexpected then, that it should have been his deliberate action which introduced the next stranger into our midst. It was, he later admitted to my mother, the only disinterested thing he had ever done for anyone and Providence had deservedly punished him for it.

He often told us of his wartime buddy, Oscar, a splendid fellow we were led to believe – after all he was Mac's friend – who made no secret of his German descent. Indeed his full name, Oscar Fiedler, would have made it difficult.

'When an enemy plane flew over everyone used to say "Look out Fiedler, here comes one of your relations!" He didn't mind. He'd just laugh. Great chap.'

It was arranged that the 'great chap' should come and spend a Sunday afternoon with us.

He came. He not only stayed to tea but, by general request, stayed on to supper. He and Mac of course had their wartime experiences in common while my father was immediately won over by the fact that, on coming out of the army, he had decided to make singing his career and was studying in London to become an operatic baritone. He also played cards. What more could one ask?

When he had at last gone Mac looked round at us in triumph.

'I told you he was a good chap, didn't I?' he said. He did, we assured him, and he was.

Oscar came the following Sunday and stayed on after supper. The Sunday after that he came and played tennis, then stayed on for another evening of cards, and the third Sunday they went on so late that he missed the last train and we put him up for the night. After that his gradual absorption into the household was just a matter of natural progression. Very soon his few belongings were transferred to Captain Wilson's old room and he was joining in the general bedlam of double dummy bridge, argument and table tennis that was by now the Melton lifestyle.

Like Mac, Oscar was essentially a product of the first war; though the effects on him had been slightly different, the most obvious being that it had turned him into a compulsive cigarette smoker. He lit each one from the last, generally when it was not much more than half burned, and suffered from such an irrational fear of running out that he hid packets about the house – from himself; my father smoked a pipe and Mac preferred another brand – in case an earthquake or tidal wave should cut him off from the nearest tobacconists. He would never admit to himself how many he smoked in a day. It was the only subject in the world that he was not prepared to discuss.

Naturally this particular foible was looked upon with indulgence by Mac and my father; in fact Oscar fitted very well into the essentially male-orientated household. With his coming the pace even accelerated. The games of table tennis grew louder and more violent and at weekends started immediately after breakfast. He would play with a kind of frenzied concentration, broken by fits of uncontrollable laughter, when the veins stood out on the side of his head and he seemed only just this side of apoplexy.

My recollection of this time is that a kind of dotty euphoria overcame us all. It was as though a madder and madder gaiety prevailed, shouts of triumph from the victorious or the flow of picturesque oaths that were the only words of German that Oscar actually knew rang through the house most of the day. Crown and Anchor became the rage – even that last resort of imbecility, Put-and-Take, now happily as long forgotten as the game of Beaver – anything that one could bet on and where money could change hands. In the now battle-scarred drawing-room the ping-pong table remained permanently up. All superfluous ornaments or picture frames had long since been smashed or swept aside. Ordinary standards of sanity were forgotten and wet weekends became a kind of prolonged mayhem.

Yet if this was the manic side of the picture, there was inevitably the depressive. One such occasion sticks in my mind. It is Saturday evening and the monotonous repetition of the table-tennis ball is stilled at last, the bats flung down anywhere. There is a blessed, if temporary, lull. Oscar, defying the unwritten male code of the house, is in the dining-room helping my mother lay the supper table while Mac and my father, by the drawing-room fire, are continuing the perpetual game of 'double-dummy', humming to themselves and muttering in the stream-of-consciousness jargon of all card players.

Mac (singing): 'There's a picture for you'. He throws down the card.

My father looks thoughtful, scratches his chin before replying: 'Hm! Ain't the bigguns large, eh? Ain't the bigguns large? You know you've got the luck of Old Nick, you have! I reckon if you fell down a drain you'd come up with a pearl necklace.'

Crouching unnoticed behind the battered sofa, my hands smelling of dusty carpet and lead soldiers, I continue to study Tom Webster's Annual. I know all their patter. I've heard it a hundred times.

My father, chanting, thoughtfully: 'I've got a little one . . .'
Mac (ditto): 'He's got a little one . . . '

Both, in unison: 'Oompta, oompta, oompta tay.' This is normal stuff, as safe and familiar as the ticking of the drawing-room clock. One only starts to listen, spine tingling with apprehension, when the voices begin to rise. Very soon they do.

'Just a moment. You trumped my heart from dummy just now, remember.'

'I did not!'

'Excuse me!'

'All right then, call me a liar. Go on – call me a liar!'

Behind the sofa I'd freeze, like a partridge in stubble, praying that I should escape detection and remain out of it. Then would come the chair pushed back, Mac's rapid strides and the slamming of the door followed by an angry, overcharged silence.

For the rest of the evening each would ostentatiously sit in a separate room. Later Mac would seek the opportunity to say to my mother in his most casual, throw-away manner, 'I think that husband of yours is going just a little bit barmy, Norah dear. I do hope you don't mind.'

Upstairs in their bedroom my father would say for the hundredth time, 'That chap really will have to go, Norah. I will not have him about the place any longer.'

Next morning the card table would once again block the way to the dining-room fire and when my mother called out that lunch was waiting there would be the usual response, 'Just a minute dear – when we've finished this hand.'

Life, then, continued on the surface much as before the advent of Oscar, though at an increasing tempo. Yet his coming inevitably changed the chemical content, the 'mix'. One would have thought that the situation already contained sufficient imbalance to cause severe strains and unspoken tensions, as it clearly did; yet it was not until the coming of Oscar that these latent dangers seemed to be activated. With his arrival allegiances changed, the balance of power ever so slightly shifted. It was as though he represented that single, portentous note that heralds an impending change of key.

One day after Mac had set off for Croydon aerodrome on his Norton, Oscar, watching from one of the upstairs windows, said quietly to my mother, 'I hope Mac's plane crashes and is smashed into a thousand little pieces.'

The days of Melton were already numbered.

Chapter XXII
The Last Sunday Lunch

The events of reality have a way of unfolding themselves in a manner that would put the ordinary purveyor of fiction on the breadline very quickly. There are seldom any of the big confrontation scenes, the fine clear-cut issues that make for good drama. The turning-points of one's life may come and go unnoticed, only to be recognized for what they were many years later. By that time it could well be too late to form a fair critical judgement of their causes. The databank of one's mind can only produce answers from what it is fed upon; and what one feeds it has been unconsciously edited and re-edited over the years.

I supposed everyone concerned must have known in their hearts, if they'd stopped to think – which of course was the last thing they intended to do – that some sort of disaster or domestic crack-up was bound to come in the end. It finally came one Sunday lunchtime.

My mother was spending a day in bed. This in itself was so extraordinary that it needs some explanation. She had recently had a great many teeth out, possibly as an agreeable alternative to life at Melton; and with this alibi had abandoned the rest of us to our fate.

We were an all-male party round the broken dining-room table downstairs; my father, carving the Sunday joint, Mac,

Oscar, my brother and myself. None of us, of course, had any idea that it was the last time we should all be gathered together in such a way.

The meal began unsensationally with my father, standing with some difficulty to carve, his two sticks propped conveniently against the arms of his chair. He was in an expansive mood, which made the process of carving even slower than usual, and was describing to us a new block of flats he had recently been over in London. One of the things that struck him as novel, he said, was that the overflow pipe from the bath went straight out on to the bathroom floor.

Pausing, he looked at my brother and myself. 'Do either of you boys want some red gravy?' Then to me, 'Come on – boy' – the name was on the tip of his tongue – 'Make you as strong as a tiger in a fit.'

My brother was still puzzled. 'But Dad,' he said, 'what's the sense of the overflow pipe going on to the floor?'

'What do you mean, boy?' my father answered, then beckoning in my direction, 'Come on, come on, pass up your plate.'

'But if it was going to overflow on to the floor anyway, why bother to put a pipe?'

My father was clearly nettled at this, especially as, across the table, Oscar was beginning to go purple and Mac's pale potent eyes to glint with prospective malice.

Feeling his position as head of the house and an authority on building matters challenged, my father turned with dignity on my brother and said: 'I'm not saying it was a good idea or a bad idea. I'm merely saying that is how it was.' Then, as a crushing addition: 'Please allow me to know what I'm talking about, my boy.'

So far nothing had been said that might not have been heard at any number of Sunday dinner tables up and down the Cornwall Road or anywhere else. All might still have been well if Mac had not stepped in. Looking immensely serious and respectful – always a danger signal – he leant towards my father and said, 'But Steph, wouldn't it be even better to have an overflow pipe that went round and emptied itself back into the bath again? I mean wouldn't that save the mess on the bathroom floor?'

To our shame we laughed – openly. The unaccustomed position of having Mac as an ally, no longer to be his selected butt and victim, went to our heads; the ties of blood and family obligations were forgotten. We vied with each other to make even sillier suggestions.

'Why not have a pipe going back up into the water tank?' we crowed.

'Or out on to the roof!'

'Or down the stairs and out of the front door.'

'All right, all right,' shouted my father, above the rising tide of idiocy, 'you can laugh, but you don't any of you know what you're talking about.'

By now the whole situation was completely out of control. Upstairs in her bedroom my mother heard the laughter begin, first as a mere family zephyr, but soon rising to gale force. In vain she listened for her husband's voice among those laughing; its absence told her all she needed to know.

Presently, above the sounds of hysteria in the dining-room,

she heard the slip-slop of his footsteps as he dragged himself upstairs towards the bedroom.

I don't know what was said. I have no desire to know. Many blanks I should very much like to fill in; not that one. I have no clear recollection of what finally happened. It was all so undramatic, so apparently normal. My mother was to go back to her parents for a time, until she was completely well again. My father went round to stay with his commuter friend, Mr Flower, my brother and I went in next door with Aunt Mabel and Uncle Ath. By the following Sunday the sound of the gramophone and the ping-pong ball had been stilled for ever. Melton was empty.

Chapter XXIII
When Did You Last See Your Father?

The realization that our life as a family unit was over came to me only very slowly. Nobody ever said it in so many words. Perhaps it was not at first the intention that it should be so. A possible explanation may be first that, what had begun simply as an off-the-cuff reaction to an increasingly intolerable situation, was allowed to harden, as the days went by, into a permanency.

No doubt my mother, rescued in the nick of time, as my grandparents must have felt, and recuperating in the comparative sanity of Kensington Gore, was prevailed upon to give up the struggle, admit defeat and face the fact that her marriage had finally broken down. No doubt, too, the realization, or at least the admission, came only slowly as the influence of Melton dwindled.

Back in Belhaven the summer trickled by. Mac had found himself digs nearer Croydon aerodrome; where Oscar went I don't know. My brother was sent off to boarding-school – presumably at my grandparents' expense, because nobody else could have paid for it; least of all my father, now an exile in Old Blossom's household, only a quarter of a mile away. From the windows of Belhaven one could see the empty garden next door, the garden of my father's rose pergolas and Captain Wilson's nine-hole golf course, gradually going to seed, the grass uncut, weeds forcing their way up through the crazy paving, and the privet hedge sprouting like an unshaven chin.

Everybody was very kind. It must have been something of a strain on the family next door to have landed upon them an extra inmate, five years older than their own son. And, of course, the situation was complicated by the fact that Uncle Ath, as my father's elder brother, must naturally have seen things very differently from Pix; not only my mother's sister but her intimate and confidante as well. I remember, then, no recriminations, no arguing. I was never made to feel unwanted or a nuisance; yet what I chiefly remember is an indefinable drop in mental status. I became, in my own mind, not a son but a nephew. At the end of meals I would get up virtuously from the table and help carry the empty plates into the kitchen while my cousin, five years younger than myself but the son of the house, would be on the sofa reading the *Rainbow*. (Only a lifelong nephew, one may add, would notice and remember such a thing.)

It was a strange summer. It was as though one had reached a point of complete stillness, after moving in one direction, before gathering speed to go in reverse. My father, a quarter of a mile or so away in the next road, and I were the last vestigial remnants of what had once been our family. It should have brought us together. It didn't. Suppressing my conscience I'd put off as long as possible the evening visit I knew I should pay him until I would eventually find myself alone in a room with Uncle Ath and we would both know what was in the other's mind.

Moving one of the Cornish marble vases on the mantel-shelf a fraction of an inch he would say casually, 'Have you been round to have a word with your Dad lately, old fellow?'

I knew he hated having to say it and that it was duty as an uncle rather than affection as a brother that forced him to do so.

'Well, not this week, actually,' I would answer, hoping he didn't remember that it was at least a fortnight.

'I daresay you've got lots to do, of course – prep and so on – but I think I would, old chap, if I were you. It's a bit lonely for him, I should think, and I'm sure he'd be jolly pleased to see you.'

I think Old Blossom's family must have tactfully retreated whenever I went round. I would find my father, just as he used to be on the summer evenings at Melton, in a deckchair in the garden, not reading but staring into the distance, while from the next-door gardens came the sound of hand-pushed lawn mowers, their knives spinning free as they turned for the next cut, and the voices of evening tennis players cheerfully calling the score farther down the road.

Old Blossom's garden was not like the one at Melton. It was a simple, basic rectangle, consisting almost entirely of an area of ill-kept grass surrounded by small, ill-kept flowerbeds; for Old Blossom was just beginning to enjoy the full fruits of his bankruptcy and no longer felt the need to keep up with the Joneses or anybody else and was therefore, unlike the rest of his world, free to neglect his garden and play golf as much as he liked.

By this time the true situation, or something vaguely like

it, had seeped through into my twelve-year-old intelligence. Naturally this made things even more awkward for both of us. My father would generally start off with what was clearly intended to be taken as a Manly Determination Not to Refer to Certain Topics.

'Well, my boy,' he would say, with determined cheerfulness, 'and what have you been up to since I last saw you, eh?'

A simple enough question you'd think, even though it did contain a suggestion, well-merited, that he hadn't seen me for a long time. But I soon learned that it was not as simple as it seemed. The great difficulty lay in knowing how to make a reply that didn't give him one of the openings that I soon came to realize he was working for. But he'd got you either way. If one said, 'Oh, nothing much,' hoping to imply that I was having no more fun than he was, he would answer: 'Never mind. One day, when my luck changes, perhaps I can take you about a bit. Go to Wimbledon or the Oval together, eh? How about that?'

And when one had thanked him in advance he would sigh and say, 'Oh, well, one day perhaps, who knows!'

Or if I was unwise enough to admit that I'd been up to London to see my mother and that she'd taken me to a matinée of *Treasure Island*, a look of pain would come over his face and he'd say: 'Oh, well, one day, when my ship comes home, perhaps I shall be able to do as much for you as your mother can.'

There was really nothing one could say to this. We would both feel embarrassed, while over the fence the mower whirred and the score went from forty-thirty to deuce.

After a while he'd say, 'Oh, by the way, do you think you'll be seeing your mother this week?'

This was difficult. All my twelve-year-old reflexes registered danger.

'I don't really know,' I'd reply, feebly playing for time.

'I was only going to say, if you do happen to, you might tell her that I've seen the doctor again and he's fairly pleased with me. If she'd be interested, that is. Think you can remember that?'

'You've seen the doctor again and he's pleased with you.'

'Fairly pleased with me.' He could make it sound like a sentence of death. 'Only if you happen to be seeing her, of course.'

Having said this he would very obviously Change the Subject by saying: 'Well, now let's talk about something else, shall we? How have you been getting along at school since I last saw you? How's the work going, eh?'

It was the messages and their implications that I learned to dread the most, because I knew, though nobody actually told me, that I was the last line of communication between my parents. It was as though a relationship that had begun with such high, romantic hopes long ago in my grandfather's drawing-room was fizzling out in a game of chess by correspondence, but a horribly important game to all concerned, with myself as the postcard that went between them.

Of course I knew that I had a great responsibility in how I reported each to the other. Naturally when I next saw my mother she'd question me closely – 'How did he seem? What exactly did he say?' and so on – and I knew that she was searching the rather bald and feeble accounts I gave her of our meetings for clues to my father's state of mind and health. And I also knew that if I'd given her a really full and true account, with all his inevitable bids for sympathy, she would have been furious with him for trying to play on my feelings, and would quite probably have forbidden me to go and see him, which, though it would have been a relief in one way, would have been difficult in another.

So, not surprisingly, I developed a kind of built-in safety device – a censorship mechanism – when speaking of each to the other that soon became second nature.

But on later consideration it's possible that I over-dramatize my role all those years ago in Old Blossom's garden. After all, it would not be a surprising thing for any child of my father's to do. Besides, children always like to feel they are playing an important part in grown-up affairs.

On the whole I think my assessment of the situation was probably pretty accurate, because every now and then my father would give up all pretence of any stoicism and say, straight out, 'It's a bit hard for a man at my time of life when even his wife and children turn against him.'

I would stand there, shuffling from one foot to the other, mentally looking at my wrist-watch and trying unsuccessfully to think of something to say. I couldn't. In a way I agreed with him – we all did – it was hard. At last the blessed moment, which he must have wanted as much as myself, would come for me to say goodbye and, once clear of the front gate, skip off in the direction of the Cornwall Road, jumping on and off the curb as I went in an access of release – a child again.

I don't blame either of my parents for that summer. Which of us could be certain that, in the same circumstances, we would have done any better? But one feels that there are certain lessons to be learned from it. First of all I feel that in most cases children should stick to one parent only. This, of course, will be quite unfair to the other because in any failed marriage it must be very unusual for the blame to be solely on one side. This whole question, though, of taking sides, of apportioning blame and guilt, is something that, in my opinion, children should be spared. The responsibility is too great. They don't want it. The whole thing is too much for them. In fact it is unnatural. Children, one feels, see things to some extent in simple black and white. There are still heroes and villains. They should take sides. The fine distinctions of balanced judgement are too subtle and mature – too worrying.

If this seems too arbitrary, too grossly weighted on one side to the detriment of the other, remember that it is not the children's fault – and in any case the losing parent may comfort himself – or herself – with the thought that in adolescence the child will most probably change sides.

Villains will becomes heroes, and vice versa. Judgements will be turned upside down, on principle.

Naturally enough when two people split up they instinctively compete for the affection of the children; yet it is this competition, this conflict of allegiance, which I believe does the damage.

All of which was no doubt beginning to seep into my mother's mind during this long summer because somehow, I don't remember how or why, my visits to Old Blossom's back garden just quietly ceased. Maybe I only went a few times, and time and memory have exaggerated their number. If that is so then it merely goes to prove my point. At any rate one evening, when we'd at last finished trying to find something to say to each other and I'd felt again that sense of liberation – liberation from the adult world of unhappiness, blame and ill-will – and bounced out of Old Blossom's front gate it was for the last time.

I have no recollection of the occasion.

Postscript

The small space between this chapter and the last represents a time lapse of twenty-seven years.

I had not seen my father since I last left him, all those years ago, sitting in Mr Flower's garden. We had carried on a desultory correspondence at such times as Christmas or birthdays – meaningless duty letters that said nothing of what we thought or felt, though there was one, I remember, written during the war, which advised me to 'continue to grow as many veg. as you can. You'll never regret it.' That was the only piece of parental advice I can remember him giving me.

During that twenty-seven years Captain Wilson had disappeared without trace and was still, one hoped, managing to keep one jump ahead of retribution; Mac, true to his creed, had gone on flying when nature and his failing nerve warned him to stop, and had been killed in an air crash. Oscar had married my mother.

For the purposes of this story the venue is now many miles from the Cornwall Road, though the exact place is unimportant. One morning my wife handed me an envelope addressed in a careful but unfamiliar handwriting. The letter inside was written on a small piece of lined paper torn from a block. It said, briefly, that my father was ill and not expected to live many days. The solicitors, it said, had advised that the family should be told, but the writer could find no other address but mine. It was signed 'E. M. Wood (Miss), Housekeeper'.

The phone number had been written clearly at the top. The exchange was one of those Surrey villages that had figured so largely in Uncle Ath's beagling anecdotes of the past – though no longer recognizable as such, no doubt.

It seemed strange that by an act as simple and mundane as lifting a telephone receiver one could break a silence that had lasted from childhood to middle age and had become such a built-in part of one's life – that one could so lightly acquire, if only briefly, something as fundamental as a father.

The voice at the other end – presumably E. M. Wood (Miss), Housekeeper – was practical and without emotion. I might have been a regular enquirer merely asking for the latest news. She thanked me for ringing and told me, without comment, that since writing to me my father had become worse and was not now expected to live many hours. I told her that I'd get in touch with my mother and my brother and that we'd get there as soon as we could.

'Oh, yes,' she said. 'Would you care to come to lunch?' She made it sound as though dropping in for lunch every twenty-seven years was perfectly normal.

I said we'd come as soon as possible afterwards.

The bungalow, when we found it, was in a quiet cul-de-sac, a private road set in a small garden full of shrubs and climbing roses. It was vastly better than Melton.

The door was opened by a thin, anxious-looking cockney woman, much younger that I had expected. Yes, he was still alive, but unconscious. He had seemed to understand, earlier, when she told him we were coming and she thought he was pleased.

I confess that I was extremely interested to see E. M. Wood (Miss) – presumably the 'Emily' referred to occasionally in my father's letters. She had come to look after him, many years before – straight from school one would have thought; she was still quite a young woman – and had actually been with him almost as long as had my mother; though, one assumed, in a different capacity. I was expecting a hard-bitten middle-aged woman, resentful of the family who had, in her eyes, neglected him for twenty-seven years, only to turn up on the doorstep in time to claim what was coming to them. Her practical manner and lack of emotion on the telephone certainly fitted into the pattern; yet somehow the vision of her in the flesh did not. Clearly she was not hard – anxious, yes, but not hard – yet how was it she seemed so lacking in emotional commitment? One felt that this cockney woman was the last means by which one might catch a reflected glimpse, however brief, of my father's character in its final phase.

She invited us in. The room was small but scrupulously clean and full, much too full, of objects that were originally wedding presents or which my father had designed for his first home; once familiar objects of our family life and now totally forgotten. There were the blue-and-white jugs he had bought at Porlock, on their honeymoon, and a silver cigarette box with a hunting scene on the lid that had been on one of the occasional tables in the drawing-room until the final era of table tennis swept it into limbo. Most significant of all, a silver epergne. This, also a wedding present, of an elaborate, convoluted design and no apparent function, was an object that had somehow come to epitomize my parents' marriage. My father greatly admired it while my mother disliked it so passionately that she would never allow it to be visible. Now it stood defiantly polished and tended, presumably by Emily, in the centre of the table.

Was this a gesture? It could well have been, yet Emily's manner belied it. She seemed pleased, almost relieved, that my mother had come and that she was no longer the only woman coping with a situation that was outside her experience.

'Would you like to go straight in and see him?' she said. My mother went in first, followed by my brother. It was a small room and, with Emily, they more or less filled it. I waited in the doorway, watching my mother's face to try to warn myself in advance of what I might see. It was a moment I had thought about and unconsciously dreaded since I was a boy of thirteen.

When it came it seemed unexpectedly small and inadequate. A very, very old man lay propped up in bed, his head sagging forward. The lower part of his face, without teeth, was so sunken and emaciated as to be almost shapeless. One could see no trace of familiarity. There was nothing to connect him with the figure of my father, straw-hatted, sitting in the back of an open cab on his way to the golf club; my father, his bow tie askew, playing 'double-dummy' with Mac in the back room at Melton. This was just an old, old man – any old man – in the last few hours of his life.

Somehow this came as a great relief. It was less personal that way.

Afterwards Emily insisted that we stay for a cup of tea. One felt it would have been churlish to refuse. Seeing my mother and Emily together it seemed odd that these two extremely ill-assorted women should be joined together in spirit by a common sharing, though presumably not on equal terms, of my father. Somewhere in the air one felt, not an antagonism but an unconscious sympathy.

Eager as ever for scraps of information, my mother questioned her closely about the last few years of my father's life.

'Oh, he seemed happy enough playing his patience and doing his jigsaw puzzles,' she said. 'Quite quiet, he was always. But the best times was when old Mr Blossom used to come and stay. There – I shouldn't call him that I suppose. He and the Old Gentleman used to sit till all hours talking over old times.' ('Old Gentleman' indeed!) 'Always seemed to cheer him up when Mr Blossom as I call him came over. When he died I think that kind of upset the Old Gentleman. Well, it was the last one I suppose, in a way. But I liked old Mr Blossom. A real dear old fellow, he was.'

And her little dark eyes suddenly filled with tears – but not for my father.

That night, after I'd arrived home, Emily rang to say my father had died soon after we left. The funeral would be on Saturday at ten-thirty.

A very ancient Rolls-Royce, smelling strongly of death, stood outside the bungalow this time when I arrived. My brother was already there. Emily had brought her mother, a shrewd-looking, hard little woman in black who wouldn't have seemed out of place in the back streets of an Italian city, and who took over the whole proceedings.

'There,' she said, when she saw my brother. 'The very image of the Old Gentleman.' Turning to Emily: 'Isn't he the very image?'

One felt she'd prepared the speech before my brother left home.

The chief undertaker, owl-like, with a mop of dark hair and glasses to match his suit, flitted in and out with soundless professional woe. One felt like saying to him, 'It's all right, mate, you needn't bother to be so gloomy about this one.' It probably wouldn't have made any difference.

'Have you given the men a drink?' Emily's mother whispered audibly to her. 'They'll expect it. They always do.' One felt she was a veteran of many such occasions. And when Emily, flustered, suggested my father's precious whisky, she said: 'Oh no – gin. That's what they generally have. Gin. They can't expect whisky. Oh no. Whatever next?'

It was soon clear that, in the absence of my mother, Emily had transferred her allegiance to my brother. A black tie was ironed ready for him. To my extreme surprise he put it on. She had also looked him out a little parcel of keepsakes.

Only three of us attended the service: Emily, a black cockney wisp, twitching with nerves, trotted beside my brother to the ancient Rolls, while I drove behind, alone, through the anonymous streets of south London to the anonymous crematorium. It seemed a small result for seventy-odd years of living – just my brother, myself and Emily. And yet perhaps this is the way it should be. Perhaps we should spend the latter part of our lives shedding, not acquiring.

We were the first party of the day. Inside all was tactfully impersonal and only perfunctorily ecclesiastic. It might as well have been a hotel lounge or a hospital waiting-room. The young undertaker with the owl-glasses motioned us into the front pew with a beautifully controlled movement of one eyebrow. One wondered whether he practised it at home. Anyway, he needn't have bothered. Seating was no problem with only the three of us.

It only took a few moments. Afterwards, as we were going out, I saw Emily, tidy to the last, slip back into her pew and rehang the kneeler on its hook for the next lot. For some reason it warmed one's heart a little.

Outside, as we got into our cars, another meagre procession was already waiting at the gates to come in. The driver of the hearse gave one very discreet hoot on his horn, like a footman coughing. These things have to be timed to a split second.

My brother and Emily disappeared into south London in the back of the Rolls. I was alone. It was still only about a quarter to ten on a Saturday morning. On a sudden impulse I stopped a passer-by and asked the way to Sutton. If I had failed to rediscover my father in the final moments of his life then surely the place to seek him was in his natural habitat, the Cornwall Road. Impelled by a number of unexpectedly strong emotions, the chief of which was no doubt guilt, I set off.

The distance from Croydon to Sutton, measured in miles, cannot be great; yet in time it can be light years. I was never conscious of passing any familiar landmarks yet, as I drove, something seemed to be happened to my surroundings.

Gradually they took on a faintly nightmarish familiarity. This must be the road up which my father's cab used to clop from Sutton station in the afternoons. But it was not the things that had changed that gave it a strange look, because they were surprisingly few; it was the things that I had last seen with a child's eye and which had become gradually transformed in my mind over the years until my memories of them were more real than the actuality. This road up which I was driving, with its laurel and privet hedges, seemed somehow unconvincing, like a badly painted back-cloth, yet I knew in my mind that this was Sutton and the scene of my childhood rather as one knows in dreams the name of a person though he bears no resemblance to him in real life.

It was now well into the morning, but there seemed to be not a soul about. I stopped a moment outside that first house which had epitomised my father's highest hopes and ambitions. The rather grandiose double gates with their elaborate posts were still much as before, though the name on them had been changed. Yet as I looked I discovered under about five layers of dark paint a beaten metal plate. One could still just trace, in the elongated, 'artistic' lettering of 1907 so beloved of my father, the name they had given it and which by now must have been completely forgotten.

The dream-like feeling was even stronger when, a moment later, I reached the Cornwall Road. There were those twin horrors, Melton and Belhaven, completely unaltered. Even their meaningless names were still the same. There was the front door with its stained-glass panels. There was the back yard that was such a formidable hazard in Captain Wilson's

nine-hole golf course. One almost expected to see the ominous Norton motor cycle with its dreaded rider setting off for
Croydon aerodrome or my father with his two sticks and his
bowler at an angle, stepping out of his cab.

Yet nobody came. There was an almost unnatural stillness
about it all. Standing there in that place so saturated in memories of childhood one had the uncomfortable feeling that, if
the front door had opened and somebody had come out, they
would have walked straight by, or even through, me. It was I,
not what I saw, that was unreal.

In a sudden revulsion against this whole business of raking
up the past I jumped into my car, crashed the gears and began
driving – anywhere that would take me as far away as possible
from the Cornwall Road.

I have never been back there since.

SLIGHTLY FOXED EDITIONS

Slightly Foxed Limited

53 Hoxton Square, London N1 6PB

tel 020 7033 0258 · fax 0870 1991245

all@foxedquarterly.com · www.foxedquarterly.com